6.50

D0015808

The Seattle School
2510 Elliott Ave.
Seattle, WA 98121
theseattleschool.edu

WITHDRAWN

The Seattle School

10028526

Prophecy and History in
Luke–Acts

Prophecy and History in Luke–Acts

DAVID L. TIEDE

FORTRESS PRESS   PHILADELPHIA

Biblical quotations from the Revised Standard Version of the Bible, copyright 1946, 1952, © 1971, 1973 by the Division of Christian Education of the National Council of the Churches of Christ in the U.S.A., are used by permission.

COPYRIGHT © 1980 BY FORTRESS PRESS

All rights reserved. No part of this publication may be reproduced, stored in a retrieval system, or transmitted in any form or by any means, electronic, mechanical, photocopying, recording, or otherwise, without the prior permission of the copyright owner.

Library of Congress Cataloging in Publication Data

Tiede, David Lenz.
    Prophecy and history in Luke-Acts.

    Bibliography: p.
    Includes indexes.
    1. Bible. N.T. Luke and Acts—Criticism, interpretation, etc. I. Title.
BS2589.T53   226′.406   79–8897
ISBN 0–8006–0632–9

8032A80   Printed in the United States of America   1–632

*He also said to the multitudes, "When you see a cloud rising in the west, you say at once, 'A shower is coming'; and so it happens. And when you see the south wind blowing, you say, 'There will be scorching heat'; and it happens. You hypocrites! You know how to interpret the appearance of earth and sky; but why do you not know how to interpret the present time?"
(Luke 12:54–56)*

Contents

CONTENTS

Acknowledgments

Without the support and cooperation of a broad network of institutions, colleagues, and family, the intense leisure which an academic sabbatical affords for the pursuit of such efforts as this volume represents would not be possible. The president, faculty, boards, and supporting constituencies of Luther and Northwestern Theological Seminaries, the Aid Association for Lutherans' program for faculty support, and the Lutheran Brotherhood grant for sabbatical assistance administered by the Division for Theological Education and Ministry all contributed to making the year possible. The Society of Biblical Literature and Institute for Antiquity and Christianity in close cooperation with the Claremont Graduate School and the School of Theology in Claremont furnished privileged access to the faculties, students, and libraries in a stimulating academic community through the SBL Fellow in Residence program in Claremont. A great personal debt to many friends, colleagues, and former teachers is also acknowledged, especially to those who extended their encouragement, critiques, and endorsements when the project was still in its early stages. But above all, this volume is dedicated in gratitude to the person who interrupted her own career at an inopportune time and graciously endured my preoccupation, absence, alternating dismay and elation, and endless reports on the current state of this project: my friend and wife, Muffy.

1

The Narrative Gospel

The Days of Vengeance

For people identified with the Jewish nation in the Roman empire, the last third of the first century was a time of intense physical and psychological suffering, a time that required the reformation of long-standing theological traditions and the reconstitution of the community of "Israel" under great stress. The calamitous revolt against Rome (A.D. 66–73) which resulted in the destruction of the sacred temple and the decimation of the Palestinian population marked a turning point in this painful process. But the war was neither the beginning nor the end of the gathering of external forces that appeared bent on the annihilation of Jewish faith and life or of the internal struggle over the causes of such distress and the understanding of what was now to be expected. The question of God's apparent desertion of the people was pressed urgently upon all who would speak of divine justice, mercy, or involvement in human affairs. Although such issues had long been debated among widely divergent Jewish groups and theological traditions in the era of the second temple, with its destruction, the continued existence of the people of Israel was of immediate and practical concern and competing views became increasingly more difficult to accommodate. As always, the vanquished were pitted against each other and burdened with the question, "Why?"

The poignancy of the question was only increased by the knowledge that the forces of destruction had been gathering for decades.

1

Calls to arms had been evoked by oppressive taxation and disregard for sacred practices and institutions while pleas for patience in the face of the awesome power of the Roman legions were also still vividly etched in the popular memory. Could the denouement of this tragic tale have been different? Or was this sadly predictable course of events simply unavoidable? Where was the point of no return, the critical moment when the fate of the city and its people was sealed? Was there, finally, no way to appease the powers, to avert the vengeance of Caesar and of God? Was some larger fate or necessity or justice served by this grim history? Then what of God and God's people in the world? Where was God's justice, let alone divine mercy? Was Israel's faith in the promises of God all in vain?

The pathos of such questions can only be appreciated by recognizing the multiplicity and intensity of efforts of the Jewish people to be faithful to their heritage in the years of Roman rule. Long recognized and frequently resented as peculiar in the world of the hellenistic empires, the Jews had been accorded special legal status by Caesar Augustus. But that recognition also occasioned violent attacks in diverse locations when official respect and protection declined. Philo of Alexandria's account of his humiliating embassy to Gaius Caligula in order to plead for the protection of the law, the dramatic resistance of the Jews in Palestine to Caligula's order to have his effigy erected in the temple, and the inauguration of the "Jewish tax," as well as efforts to reduce the legal rights of the Jews in Alexandria and Antioch after the war are all familiar examples of the persistent pressure associated with that special status.[1] Furthermore, the insensitive and often incitive administration of Roman policy by several of the procurators in Palestine made political solutions to their worsening plight less and less available. Of course, the situation was considerably more complex than this hasty review would suggest. In retrospect, however, even the Roman historian Tacitus, who had no affection for the Jews, granted that "the Jews patiently endured their fate until Gessius Florus became governor" (A.D. 64–66). Then, as Josephus acknowledged, the Jews were "constrained to take up war with the Romans, for we preferred to perish together rather than by degrees."[2]

Up to the end of the war, and in some instances well beyond it,

2

the several parties perceived themselves as faithful Israel and struggled to express their steadfast obedience to God even at extreme peril or the cost of their lives. Yohanan ben Zakkai fled the besieged city in a coffin in order, as Jacob Neusner suggests, "to devise a program for the survival and reconstruction of the Jewish people and faith."[3] The pious sectarians, who had withdrawn to the wilderness of the Dead Sea to avoid the contamination of Jerusalem and to anticipate the intervention of God, were simply overrun by the invading Romans. The Zealots held on at Masada and maintained careful ritual observances until the cruel end (A.D. 73). Even opportunists such as Josephus, who fled into the arms of the Romans, could recite the history of Israel within earshot of the wall of the besieged city, calling for repentance from "warring not against the Romans only, but also against God."[4] Many of the people were probably swept along by the course of events without identifying strongly with any particular political program or theological viewpoint. But Josephus also tells of the six thousand who died in the flames of the temple still hoping for the dramatic signs of divine deliverance.[5] These and countless others clung desperately to the common hope of the salvation of the faithful no matter what their differences.

Of course, the Jews of the hellenistic era merely joined the larger company of those attempting to trace some correlation between their experience of forces that often seemed arbitrary, if not malevolent, and their belief in a divine economy that ultimately prevails in human affairs. Since the days of Alexander the Great (d. 323 B.C.), the eastern Mediterranean world had served as a school for nations and peoples, poets and philosophers, priests and prophets to contemplate human freedom and responsibility in the course of history, knowing full well that the whims of the emperor or tactics of an army could profane a cultus, destroy a social, economic, and political order, and enslave a people with apparent impunity. The catalog of treatises in hellenistic philosophy includes numerous titles concerned with fate, fortune, providence, chance, "the sympathy of the universe," and necessity, and it is abundantly clear that the problem of human freedom was a pervasive theological issue in diverse schools.[6] Furthermore, hellenistic historiography, particularly as it was frequently affected by the drama of the tragedians,[7] was singularly preoccupied with the ways in which the course of human events could be influenced or controlled by personal and cosmic fates and forces.

In the closing decades of the first century A.D., the question of theodicy was again raised forcefully by the confusion and distress surrounding Nero's last years; the fear, intrigue, and vicious reprisals during the year of the four emperors, which occurred in the midst of the Jewish war (A.D. 69); and the terrors that culminated in Domitian's death (A.D. 96). In reviewing the bloodshed, suffering, and confusion of A.D. 69, the gloomy Tacitus could conclude, "In short, Rome's unparalleled suffering supplied ample proof that the gods are indifferent to our tranquillity, but eager for our punishment."[8] But the more circumspect Platonist, Plutarch, reminded that many who deserved punishment and apparently escaped it, offered a fourfold apology "On the Delays of the Divine Vengeance." He allowed that, far from allowing the slowness of judgment to destroy a belief in divine providence, such delay must be understood as the granting of time for reform for those who have sinned in ignorance.[9]

Nor were the Jews unique in clinging to their ancient national stories and theological traditions in the face of assimilation by hellenistic culture. Many conquered peoples grasped and embellished their ancient heritage in order to endure with poise and courage the vicissitudes of imperial policy and the accusations of enemies. *But the people of Israel had been there before.* They had inherited, remembered, and transmitted an exceptionally rich and living collection of sacred writings. These scriptures had been composed largely in the wake of the first destruction of Jerusalem and the temple (586 B.C.), in the years of the exile under the Babylonians and Persians, but they contained still more ancient sources and memories of God's peculiar concern and intention for Israel through thousands of years. In times of peril to or loss of cultic center and geographical displacement of the people, the scriptural heritage had already provided a locus for the identity of Israel and a testimony to divine faithfulness to promises still unfulfilled. Transcribed and translated, memorized, and commented upon from a host of perspectives, supplemented with editorial comments and additional writings, many in the name of an ancient worthy, these scriptures offered a common ground for disparate Jewish groups. In seeking to interpret their own times and to

4

defend themselves against the ridicule and attacks of others, their appeal to the ancient scriptures and their prophecies was fundamental.[10]

Not that such a "biblical theology" foreclosed discussion of the painful question of theodicy or prevented bitter infighting and fault-finding in the wake of the destruction. Even the matter of which scriptures could be used to authorize theological assertions still required resolution,[11] and among the scriptures that were generally accepted, the spectrum of views of God's role in history was very broad. The near cynicism of Ecclesiastes stood in contrast to the profound mystery of the ways of God in Job. The latter chapters of Zechariah and Daniel also testified to an apocalyptic pessimism concerning redemption within the realm of human affairs.[12] However, the extensive testimony of the deuteronomistic historians, the exilic redactions of Jeremiah and Isaiah, and the wisdom traditions as applied to Israel's history required that Israel's fortunes be correlated directly to its obedience to God and that Israel's suffering be viewed as the result of failure or refusal to heed the prophets sent to it: "Because they did not heed my words, says the Lord, which I persistently sent to you by my servants the prophets, but you would not listen, says the Lord" (Jer. 29:19).[13] No doubt the force of such an indictment was also intensified by the way the successful revolt of Israel against the Syrian Greeks had been interpreted in such works as 1 and 2 Maccabees, written in imitation of the archaic style of the scriptural histories. The emphasis on obedience to the law had been maintained as the sine qua non of the salvation of Israel and of the temple in particular.[14]

Those who stood *within* this scriptural tradition, therefore, were at least provided with certain time-honored categories and theological concepts for interpreting their experience. Yet even that common ground by no means assured unanimity in the discussion. Perhaps the scriptures could be said to have provided only the critical point of departure or, at best, the agenda for denominational debate, but the particulars of the case and the mode of argumentation awaited further determination. As James A. Sanders has argued, the assessment of the actual function of such authoritative traditions must be cognizant of several variables. "The old text or tradition called upon, the historical context into which it is cited, and the hermeneutics used in doing so" will all affect the continuing appropriation of the scriptural heritage in distinct communities.[15]

Thus, in seeking to interpret the plight of "Israel" after the destruction of the temple, most Jewish groups might have agreed on the basis of the scriptures that the disaster was due to sin. But how was the sin to be diagnosed or confessed? Was it the sin of having displayed a lack of trust in God by taking up arms, along with other secret sins, and having less regard for the sacred land and the temple than the Romans themselves had? Was such unfaithfulness the cause of a "like vengeance" to that wrought by the Assyrians, so that God himself encamped with the Romans, as Josephus suggested?[16] Was Israel guilty of the idolatry and apostasy of going the way of the Gentiles? Was Israel's sin vicious opportunism, seeking to take advantage of Roman "humanity" and "restraint" when Rome appeared weakened with internal strife, as Titus, according to Josephus, indicts besieged Jerusalem?[17] Was the sin fundamentally the unavoidable manifestation of the wickedness of all humanity, which deserved condemnation, but anticipated God's eschatological redemption, as 4 Ezra and 2 Baruch interpret this second destruction in the light of the first?[18] Or was Israel's sin much more specific, that is, the culpable nonrecognition of "the King who comes in the name of the Lord. . . . and they will not leave one stone upon another in you; because you did not know the time of your visitation" (Luke 19:38,41–44)?

Nor did the scriptural content of the analyses exclude the appropriation of diverse forms of hermeneutical arguments. Even the most separatist Jewish traditions of the era of the Hellenistic and Roman empires were influenced by the hermeneutical criteria, logical categories, and rhetorical conventions of the dominant Greek culture.[19] Nor were the Jews insulated from the philosophical and religious debates concerning determinism and human freedom so common in the Greco-Roman world.[20]

Indeed, the effort to appropriate the hermeneutical categories and methods of the day to interpret the relevance of the scriptures to the current distress must be acknowledged as a mark of the vitality of Jewish religious tradition. It may have been commonly conceded to those within and without that "these are days of vengeance, to fulfil all that is written" (Luke 21:22), and the mutual recriminations may have become harsh. But for those who attempted to testify to God's activity in this history and who ventured to reconstitute Israel in the wake of the destruction, it was also a shared conviction that God still had not abandoned his people or his redemptive purpose in the midst of the present suffering in the world.

Luke–Acts: "Glory to Thy People Israel"?

Placing Luke–Acts *within* the setting of late first-century Jewish history as described above may appear to be a folly if not an affront to the Jews. It appears to be folly because in spite of extended debates concerning the identification of the author with Paul's gentile companion, Luke the physician, the tradition that this work is the "Greek" and "gentile" Gospel continues to be a widely shared assumption that affects the interpretation of "Jewish" features of the work profoundly. It seems an affront because gentile Christianity has long found the Lucan treatment of the obduracy of the Jews to be a convenient justification for its claim to the heritage of the promises to Israel, frequently at an incredibly cruel and inhuman cost to generations of Jews. Yet the contrast between "Greek" and "Jewish" may have obscured rather than disclosed the peculiar genius of the many strains of "Jewish" tradition in the "hellenistic" era.[21] Again, even if it may be correct, the assumption that "Luke" was a Gentile has made it exceptionally difficult for subsequent generations of gentile Christians to recognize that the polemics, scriptural arguments, and "proofs" which are rehearsed in Luke–Acts are part of an *intrafamily* struggle that, in the wake of the destruction of the temple, is deteriorating into a fight over who is really the faithful "Israel."*

*Even the convention of modern English usage to capitalize the words "Jewish" and "Christian" (following the University of Chicago Press *Manual of Style*) tends to reinforce a distinction which would have been alien to the experience of many first century Jews in this messianist movement. In Luke–Acts, the process has already begun by which in later eras "Christianity" and "Judaism" will define their identities largely by mutual exclusion. But in the community which Luke portrays as believing Jesus to be messiah and Lord, those of Jewish heritage regard that belief to be the mark of their fidelity to the religion of Israel. (See note 23 below.) Likewise, in the case of the noun Gentile, I have followed conventional usage and capitalization.

The Greek provenance of Luke–Acts, moreover, is clear. Although the debate continues concerning semitisms and possible traces of translation work in selected episodes or speeches, the literary style and rhetorical eloquence of the final composition are disclosed immediately in the first sentence or prologue of the Gospel as a self-conscious imitation of or commentary upon Greek literary and historiographic conventions (Luke 1:1–4). Similarly, throughout the work, the consistent use of the Greek version of the Jewish scriptures, the tendency to explain or avoid semitic words, the practice of suiting speeches to a likely historical or stereotypical situation while integrating them into the literary context, the acknowledgment of political and religious practices and figures in Greece and Asia Minor, and even the possible use of Aristotelian syllogistic arguments may all be adduced as evidence of the thoroughly hellenized environment of Luke–Acts. This two-volume work was not only written in Greek, but it was composed by an author who was conversant in and fully at home with contemporary Greek rhetoric and literary conventions.

But Luke was also at home in the synagogue. In fact, his descriptions of synagogue ritual with detailed observations on the regular use of readings from the law and the prophets for exposition and theological disputation are still among the most complete literary accounts of first-century synagogue practice available (cf. Luke 4: 16–30; Acts 13:14–43; 15:21; 17:1–4,10–11; 18:24–26). Furthermore, Luke portrayed the synagogue as the critical setting for Jesus' programmatic announcement of the reign of God with careful attention to its grounding in scriptural exposition. The author of Luke–Acts lived within the world of the hellenistic synagogue where the scriptures provided an ancient heritage, a theological vocabulary, and a set of rituals that distinguished and identified the Jews. But those scriptures also furnished a meeting ground for vigorous synagogue debates over the interpretation of new times and situations by the application of complex methods of exposition. Thus, it comes as no surprise to discover that such scriptural allusion and hermeneutical argument permeate Luke's entire narrative. Even a hasty reading of early Christian literature indicates that the hermeneutics of Jesus and his followers often produced violent reactions and frequently occasioned their expulsion from the synagogue. Yet Luke consistently took pains to depict the messianists (*christianoi*) as belonging in the synagogue and the temple, emphasizing the attentiveness of "more noble Jews" who "received the word with all eagerness, examining the scriptures daily to see if these things were so" (Acts 17:11). Therefore, the questions "What is written in the law? How do you read?" (Luke 10:26) are critical to the evangelist as well as to Jesus and his disciples.

Furthermore, the diversity that characterized those first-century synagogues is amply displayed in Luke–Acts. As early in the narrative as Luke 7, the elders of the Jews are quoted as advising Jesus that even the centurion whose slave was ill deserved consideration "for he loves our nation, and he has built us our synagogue" (7:5). Thus, Luke presents a rich ethnic, cultural, and theological mixture of Jews, Greeks, Gentiles, proselytes, God-fearers, and worshipers of God as frequenting the synagogues. According to Luke's picture, all of these identifiable groups had been drawn variously within the orbit of Jewish religion and culture and exposed to the Jewish scriptures. Yet it is not always clear exactly which "Greeks" were Jews by birth or circumcision or which were Gentiles or what the status may have been of the devout worshipers, God-fearers, or women of high standing in those "synagogues of the Jews" (cf. Acts 14:1–7; 17:1–4,10–12,17; 18:4; 19:8–10). Seen against the background of recent archaeological work on synagogues in Palestine and Asia Minor, rediscovery of Qumran and Masada, and research on Jewish culture and religion in the era of the second temple, Luke's picture of early Christianity as another Jewish denominational movement (cf. *hairesis*: Acts 24:5,14; 28:22, cf. also Sadducees 5:17, Pharisees 15:5; 26:5) claiming its place *within* the synagogue of the hellenistic era is increasingly intelligible. And while it was not Luke's purpose to record the sociology of contemporary Jewish groups, nevertheless his picture of the emergence of the Christian mission from *within* the institutions and people of Israel is greatly enhanced by the documentation of the cultural, theological, and even ethnic complexity of the synagogues of Palestine, Asia Minor, and Greece that he does furnish.

His descriptions of the several groups serve to document his view that God's promises to Israel have found their fulfillment, including their reception by a repentant Jewish people. The distinction between Jew and Gentile is consistently maintained, and there is never any suggestion that somehow a "new Israel" that includes gentile Christian believers has supplanted or displaced the Jews. As Jacob Jervell explains, "For Luke there is only one Israel," and the promises of God which were made to Israel of old are now fulfilled for this same people.[22] Thus, great caution must be exercised in any attempt to distinguish between "Christians" and "Jews." To be sure, in his account of the persistent opposition encountered by Paul in Greece, Asia Minor, and Palestine, especially as displayed by Jews before non-Jewish crowds and public officials, the term "Jew" can almost be used as a synonym for those who oppose or reject Christian preaching (e.g., Acts 9:23; 12:3,11 (Peter); 13:45,50; 14:4,19; 17:5,13; 18:5,12, and numerous cases in chapters 20–28).[23] But in addition to the obvious fact that the early chapters of Acts dramatize the acceptance of the apostles' preaching by thousands in Jerusalem who are clearly Jewish (cf. 2:41; 4:4; 5:14; 6:7), the author takes pains repeatedly to emphasize "how many thousands [myriads] there are among the Jews [*Ioudaioi*] of those who have believed, and all of them are zealous for the law" 21:20 (cf. also 13:43; 17:4,11; 18: 4,8). It is the "unpersuaded" or "unbelieving" Jews (14:4; 28:24), therefore, who generate a division among the "Jews" which is displayed before the Gentiles (cf. 14:4; 23:7), and in Luke's narrative only the gentile procurator Festus, who was not averse to humiliating the Jews, could suggest that "the whole Jewish nation" was seeking Paul's death, and without adequate cause (25:23–27). Whether the author was himself a Greek-speaking Jew who was angered and saddened by those "Jews" who defended the law so adamantly (see Paul in Romans 9–11, Galatians) or a Gentile who held the Jewish traditions in highest regard, Luke was eager to document the success of Christian preaching among the Jews in the face of great opposition.

Judged by the canons of later eras when "orthodox Christianity" was almost exclusively gentile, frequently justifying itself at the expense of the "unbelieving Jews," and when "Normative Judaism" had largely succeeded in advancing its standards for what was "Jewish," such a viewpoint may seem impossible. Luke's understanding of the Christian mission as founded in the faith of Israel and dependent upon the repentance of believing Jews has long been incomprehensible to Jews and vulnerable to being turned by Christians into an adverse view of the "origins" of the church "out of Judaism." Certainly Samuel Sandmel's view of Christianity as one of the varieties of Judaism which, along with rabbinic Judaism, managed to survive to modern times is still quite alien to most modern Jews and Christians.[24] Nevertheless, it is precisely Luke's theological conviction that the manifestation of Jesus as messiah and the extension of his reign to include the Gentiles redounded to the "glory of Israel," which both made the Christians increasingly unwelcome in the synagogue and requires that this work be considered within the context of late first-century Jewish history.

The Evangelist as Interpreter

Luke–Acts presents a reconstruction of the founding history of the Christian community that is grand in scope and distinctive in its understanding of the continuity of that history with God's saving activity in Israel's past. Luke's story of Jesus and the apostles is staged against the backdrop of the history of the empire, Roman administration of the provinces, and within the Jewish framework of the history of the world beginning with Adam, son of God.[25] The famous synchronism marking the beginning of the preaching of John the Baptizer (Luke 3:1–2) not only recalls the formula for dating the "coming of the word of the Lord" in Israel's prophetic past (e.g., Jer. 1:1–3) but also represents the appropriation of a convention of hellenistic historiography for marking a starting point in the narrative.[26] Compared with Mark's terse and often cryptic "Gospel" or even Matthew's more expansive "book concerning the genesis of Jesus Messiah," the historical sweep of the Luke–Acts "narrative" is remarkable. This is not a kerygmatic recounting of the struggle of cosmic forces so much as a biographical history disclosing the succession of the exemplary ruler and his emulators and agents, the teacher and his disciples, or the prophet and his people.[27] Luke could not be credited with the production of the Christian Antiquities in the comprehensive mode of the apology for Roman history offered by Dionysius of Halicarnassus or the defense of Jewish history by Josephus

In drafting the story of Jesus and his followers, however, the evangelist assured his community of the continuity of the Holy Spirit's activity in the long history of Israel culminating in Jesus' exaltation and the expansion of the church's mission from Jerusalem to Rome. All of this history was also authenticated by demonstrating its correspondence with the law, prophets, and psalms of the sacred Jewish scriptures. Perhaps no work since the glorious accounts of Judas and his brothers of 1 and 2 Maccabees, or the sacred history of the patriarchs or Jubilees, or the hagiography of such Jewish hellenistic romance literature as Artapanus's treatment of Moses, or the glorification of Joseph in *Joseph and Asenath* had offered such a triumphant recitation of the history of a people through the praises of its heroes and founders. *Perhaps.* At least, a host of interpretations of Luke–Acts have noted the credibility of such an assessment of Luke's narrative, whether to their delight or chagrin.[28]

Again, since Luke can be shown to have used Mark's Gospel as a literary source and since Acts offers an extensive interpretation of Paul's ministry and preaching that can be compared with Paul's own letters, any responsible historical treatment of Luke–Acts must involve careful assessments of Luke's appropriation and alteration of his sources and discriminating judgments concerning Luke's presentation of Paul and his theology.[29] Yet employing Mark as a control for interpreting Luke has not only obscured the complexity of Luke's relation to his sources;[30] it has also tended to impose a very peculiar Markan standard for what constitutes a "gospel" on the Lucan literature. Since Mark's "Gospel" has often been viewed in modern studies with some awe as a literary *novum* in which Pauline theology of the cross, Christology, and apocalyptic eschatology were variously described as the critical elements, Luke–Acts suffered from the comparison. This work appeared by contrast all the more blandly as a "historification of the kerygma," an "explanation" of history which justified gentile Christianity as the new Israel at the expense of the Jews, or even as a "theology of glory" in which the death of Jesus had been "reduced" to merely a pious martyrdom.[31] To be sure, interpreting Luke as a redaction of Mark has demonstrated that Luke's eschatology, Christology, and pneumatology are significantly different from Mark's or Paul's, but the method must be criticized for having

12

prejudged Luke–Acts on the basis of criteria that were abstracted from other early Christian books whose historical occasion and literary genre also differed sharply from Luke's.

There is no easy way to elude this methodological predicament. The alteration of sources remains one of the most reliable and demonstrable marks of authorial activity whether intentional or implicit, and any composition can be assessed much more precisely by comparison with known predecessors and the investigation of the correspondence of the depiction of historical figures with other independent accounts. In the case of Luke–Acts, moreover, the resources for such comparison are exceptionally rich. The evangelist drew upon a broad range of Jewish scriptural sources and traditions, along with Mark and other possible literary collections (e.g., Q) and Christian traditions. No single notion of an ad hoc redaction of sources to meet an eschatological crisis, christological heresy, or shift in ecclesiastical organization has proven adequate to the material.

Such an appeal to the *literary integrity* of the work in its historical setting has required the recent reconsideration of the redaction critical contributions of the 1950s, most notably Hans Conzelmann's brilliant *The Theology of St. Luke*. It has also produced a reappraisal of the literary and form critical analyses offered by Martin Dibelius and Henry J. Cadbury in the 1920s to 1940s. In addition to a wealth of recent studies on particular motifs and excellent descriptions of the schematic structure of the two-volume work, renewed efforts to describe Luke's method as a hellenistic author and scriptural interpreter have had the effect of placing Luke–Acts within the broader field of its contemporary literature. The literary character of the composition has been recognized with increasing clarity in recent studies. Efforts to demonstrate that the complete first chapters, including the formalistic prologue (Luke 1:1–4), should be considered as prefatory to the entire work[32] and the exploration of Luke 24 and Acts 28 as appropriate literary conclusions[33] reflect this recognition. Indeed, the matter of the genre of Luke–Acts, indeed of all the Gospels, has again become an open and critical heuristic question.

Literary criticism, however, remains in a somewhat uncertain state with respect to these texts. The considerable skill of the author in shaping his materials and drafting a coherent narrative still appears to draw more plaudits than precise descriptions of his methods, and the application of modern canons of literary criticism has met with reservation in the exegetical guild. Nevertheless, these diverse literary analyses are confirming the view that Luke was no mere transmitter or recorder of Christian traditions and history, although he did conserve and document that past. His exposition of the founding history is a work of considerable literary complexity, not only appropriating diverse contemporary literary forms and stylistic features but also creating recognizable end stress, irony, plot, and tragedy as well as sustained dynamics among distinct agents and actors in typical situations. Even at the level of the narrative itself, the story is by no means an uninterrupted march from triumph to triumph. The forces of reaction and disruption in the continuity of the story are considerable. At a minimum, as Norman Petersen ascertains, *"the rejection of God's agents by God's people in connection with God's sanctuaries (synagogues and temple) is the plot device by which the movement of the narrative as a whole is motivated"* (emphasis in original).[34]

Such formal or aesthetic approaches to the text need not be considered ahistorical, although they are often regarded as correctives to attempted interpretations of a document which are based strictly on its historical genesis or verifiability. Respect for the literary integrity of Luke–Acts, however, does mean that when the bent of more particularistic minds to turn to the historical context and occasions of the work can no longer be resisted, the goal is not simply to explain the text by the alteration of its sources to meet specific exigencies. As a statement or restatement of the story of Jesus and his apostles or the prophet and his people, Luke–Acts may be regarded as a document peculiar to late first-century Christianity. As such, it is concerned to identify itself *within* Jewish tradition in the context of the Greco-Roman world, and it must also be acknowledged as an interpretation of Christian origins that will continue to have paradigmatic value for succeeding generations.

Precisely because Luke–Acts has long served such an archetypal function, forming and informing subsequent Christian tradition, the historical, cultural, and religious setting of the work must be assessed as it can best be determined. For generations of interpreters with little or no sense of the existential trauma of "Israel" in its late first-century agonies of defeat, dishonor, and dissension, Luke–Acts often seemed to provide a glorious "myth of Christian beginnings."[35] As such, the literary "plot device" of rejection was misconstrued simply as a foil by which the triumph of the church was justified before God and humanity, often at the expense of "the Jews" and frequently at the expense of historical credibility. To be sure, the recognition of this literary structure serves to identify the crucial restraint or countercurrent in the flow of the narrative. But the motif of rejection, the problem of the discontinuity of faith within Israel, the apparent incongruity of the relative lack of acceptance of this messiah among his own people cannot be treated merely as a formal plot device apart from the historical occasion of the work.

Similarly, the peculiar eschatology of Luke–Acts must be assessed within the larger cultural setting of late first-century Jewish history. Much more than an ad hoc adaptation of Mark, this narrative has entered into a complex contemporary discussion of divine justice and grace, faithfulness and abandonment, vengeance and providence in Israel's recent history. The peculiar force of Luke's story can only be estimated when the prevailing question of God's faithfulness to his promises to Israel in the light of its tragic plight and the fate of Jerusalem is also articulated. Then the literary, hermeneutical and historical occasions of this two-volume work can be described more adequately.

This "story" of Luke–Acts does have a literary integrity which is not simply derived from its sources, and it is an account of the founding history of the church that has been composed within a complex historical setting. Luke's rehearsal and reconstruction of the past is perhaps best understood as an interpretation of his own times. It is written "from within" by an author who identified strongly with Jewish tradition, although his theology and perhaps his ethnic origins would have rendered his "Jewish" identity unacceptable if not inconceivable to many in the synagogue. Explicitly intended to give "assurance" to the reader and to portray the "boldness" of Christian preaching as founded in the continuing activity of the Holy Spirit, this story is also persistently attentive to interpreting the obvious discontinuities that plague this "Jewish" sectarian movement that seeks to extend its mission in the face of rejection and even persecution by both Jews and Greeks.[36] And throughout the narrative, the scriptural phrasing, allusions, and references serve to ground that story in the prior text of the promises and plan of God.

In a world where apocalyptic timetables and gnostic schemes apparently offered avenues of escape,[37] Luke's interpretation of the times was no obvious statement. Writing an account of the founding history of the church as disclosing divine providence was audacious, if not naive, especially in the face of the resistance and rejection of Christian teaching that Luke explicitly reports. His "succession narrative" or biographical history was thus a gospel for the duration, a testimony to the faithfulness of God in the vicissitudes of history, adducing the scriptures to document their fulfillment in the contested story of Jesus and his followers *within* the unlikely framework of Israel's painful humiliation.

A Note on Method

That element which threatens the continuity and coherence of a narrative is fundamental to its cogency. Whether viewed as the plot device or as the concern of the text, such a factor ought not to be too quickly explained or easily domesticated to the service of the story line lest the account be sapped of its vitality. A pretty story of the triumph of Jesus and his apostles or an ideal picture of the institutionalization of the Spirit in the church could not have produced the debate and discussion which continues to surround Luke–Acts. As the concern of rejection introduces the reader into the alien world of first-century religious polemics in which the peril of the loss of heritage is deeply felt, the "truth" of the story, or, more precisely, its power to bespeak the truth of the way things were and are, is disclosed in the force of particularity.

Thus, the often noted schematic view of history and the plan of the story may be granted. The advance of the mission from Galilee to Jerusalem and from Jerusalem to Rome (Luke 23:5; Acts 1:8) and the demonstration of the fulfillment of the scriptural prophecies throughout that movement are integral to the story line from the birth narratives in Luke 1–2 to the poignant closing episode in Acts 28. Luke–Acts is the best source for the "glorious history of the Savior and his apostles" which the church has often been tempted to use in order to document self-serving claims. But what happens to that schema if more careful attention is paid to the critical disjunctions in the story or if the undertow of the narrative is sounded at selected points? What if the identity of the "chosen people" and their vocation remain under dispute? And if that plot device or dissonance which furnishes the story with a depth and complexity to be pondered and interpreted, if not explained, is discovered to arise from the lived experience of a people, how shall the schema that points beyond such painful experience be regarded?

Eagerly anticipating more thorough literary analyses of Luke–Acts according to hellenistic and modern canons, this volume seeks to draw attention to selected points in Luke's composition where the concern of rejection is particularly crucial to the larger purposes of the narrative. A variety of selected aspects of the story no doubt could be profitably analyzed to demonstrate the way Luke brings traditional materials to the service of his literary agenda.[38] However, by their strategic placement, programmatic subject matter, and likely connection with contemporary community experience, certain texts display a profile of the rejection which qualifies the apparent schema of the narrative. In each case, the literary activity of the author can be detected and analyzed and the appropriation of scriptural traditions to interpret the subject can be documented. It will also be necessary to attempt some descriptions of the historical and religious situation that gave the subject its particular force and perhaps affected the literary form. The theological convictions implied and expressed in this literary, expository, and historical interpretive activity of the author will therefore also require reassessment.

Four closely related subjects will thus be discussed in the following chapters in the approximate order of their pertinent texts in Luke–Acts. The central questions may be stated variously: granting the sweep and pattern of Luke's biographical history or succession narrative, granting the appropriation of royal and imperial "benefactor" language for Jesus and his apostles, granting the assurance that Jesus the messiah was identified as the prophet like Moses, now exalted in glory, to give repentance and forgiveness of sins to Israel and also the Gentiles (see Acts 5:31; 11:18), then why the rejection: 1) Why is "no prophet . . . acceptable in his own country" (Luke 4:16–30; 9:51–56)? 2) Why will Jerusalem "be trodden down by the Gentiles"

(Luke 13:31–35; 19:41–44; 21:20–24)? 3) Why must Jesus be 'delivered up according to the definite plan and foreknowledge of God" (Luke 22–23)? 4) Why must the apostle be given the dour words of the prophet Isaiah, "Go to this people and say . . . you shall indeed see but never perceive" (Acts 28:23–28)? What is the literary function of such difficult passages? How are the Jewish scriptures used to identify and warrant these textual episodes? What are the views of necessity, historical causation, and divine activity that are involved? What is the traditional history of such understandings? What are the likely historical occasions in Luke's era to which his distinctive treatment may relate?

Any one of these questions could require volumes to be treated thoroughly, and this exploratory effort to demonstrate the importance of such questions to the purposes of Luke–Acts cannot pretend to be comprehensive. Furthermore, beginning with an historical reconstruction and eventually returning to the question of Luke's relevance to such historical occasions is fraught with perils of circularity and risks of obscuring the internal coherence of the text. Nevertheless, it is precisely the renewed appreciation of the literary capacity and hermeneutical methodology of this evangelist that requires a reassessment of his "foundation history" *within* an increasingly complex picture of late first-century Jewish history. Tidy redactional explanations of why Luke "changed" Mark and overly simple statements of "the purpose of Luke–Acts," whether historical, literary, or theological, have rendered it more brittle and rigidly schematic than an ancient or modern reader would likely find credible. And as Carl Braaten has succinctly noted, "the ultimate criterion of an appropriate hermeneutic is a material one; that is, does the hermeneutical method do justice to the matter to be interpreted?"[39] Consequently, this attempt to view Luke–Acts as an interpretation of its own times can only claim to have examined the narrative at junctures that appear promising for divulging something of the depth of lived experience that required such interpretation. And in order to analyze these selected readings, it appears that literary, tradition–critical, theological, and historical considerations must all be kept in view, anticipating the need for more thorough investigations in each area.

18

2

No Prophet Is Acceptable in His Own Country

Luke 4:16–30 and the Program of Luke–Acts

Luke's account of Jesus' "sermon" in Nazareth is widely recognized as programmatic of the whole two-volume work. The length and detail of the episode, its strategic placement in the narrative, which probably reflects a rearrangement of Mark's sequence, and the heavily freighted theological content of the passage are all commonly cited in support of this judgment. But how is that program to be described? Is Luke–Acts to be seen as a straightforward and schematized exposition of the glorious words of Isaiah? Certainly it is that. But what of the appalling conflict between Jesus and his audience which immediately ensues? Does this rejection merely heighten the effect of Jesus' dominion and power, or is it fundamental to the program itself? Does it not require a more complex view of the literary construction, theological outlook, and historical occasion of Luke–Acts than generally has been recognized?

Jesus' claim to embody the fulfillment of the eschatological promises of the Isaiah text could hardly be more direct: "Today this scripture has been fulfilled in your hearing." And that "today" clearly articulates Luke's eschatological conviction that the present is the arena of the deployment of the reign of God and his anointed one. Only a few chapters later, Jesus is already pointing back to what has been accomplished, using scriptural phrasing that is closely related to the first statement of the agenda: "Go and tell John what you have seen and heard: the blind receive their sight, the lame walk, lepers are cleansed, and the deaf hear, the dead are raised up, the poor have good news preached to them" (7:22). And when the attempt is made on his life, Jesus simply defies his adversaries, walking unscathed through their midst. Such features are often cited as crucial support for the view that after his temptation, Jesus' ministry was a "Satan-free" period, an almost idyllic "middle of time" during which salvation was unambiguously manifested.[1]

Yet even the most unsophisticated reader is likely to be caught short by the shocking contrast between the two halves of the story. Just when he has announced this program, Jesus appears to turn on his audience and precipitate their hatred. In response to their words of apparent approval (4:22), Jesus predicts their rejection ("you will say"), putting hostile words in their mouths and indicting them with prophetic precedent. The juxtaposition is so sharp that it tests the adequacy of any considered attempt to explain, expound, or interpret the text.

Efforts to account for the problem on the basis of what the historical Jesus might have actually said or meant have evoked elaborate speculation. Many questions about the propriety of his synagogue practice, the "selection" of his text, and the offense of his childhood past in Nazareth have been pondered in attempts to explain the unfortunate turn of events. The possibility that some historical factor related to Jesus' past or to Luke's view of the synagogue might yet be uncovered to shed light on the problem certainly cannot be excluded. But as long as so little is known concerning first-century synagogue practice independent of Luke–Acts and as long as Luke's account is not clearly established as independent of Mark, most such historical suggestions remain very difficult to substantiate.

If Mark is assumed to be a literary source for this story, then it can be argued that Luke was simply clumsy in prefacing a story of Jesus' rejection with a glorious prophetic proof text. In his eagerness to rearrange Mark in order to set up an "inaugural address" for the newly "anointed" Jesus, perhaps Luke had to resort to future tenses and predictions of what Jesus is going to do in Capernaum (v. 23)

20

when he had not yet told Mark's Capernaum stories. But then it must be noted that it is Luke who *introduced* the complicating references to Capernaum and to Elijah and Elisha escalating the conflict and *omitted* Mark's detailed report that interprets the negative response of the audience. Compared to Mark's version, the story has been stripped bare at this critical point, leaving only the expository pronouncement and anticipatory indictments to interpret the people's single inquiry: "Is not this Joseph's son?" Such "changes" are too crucial and elaborate to be discounted as simple ineptitude. The interpreter is obliged to attempt to account for such features within the composition.

Careful redaction analysis has correctly insisted that the apparent alterations of Mark be viewed as clues to Luke's purpose and has demonstrated that such comparison leads to greater appreciation of his authorial investment in the passage. But how shall that investment be described? If the Gospel of Luke is viewed as a schematized "salvation history" intended to assuage the nonappearance of the Parousia, then the apparent conflict may only be an occasion for displaying how the invincible Jesus inaugurated the reign of God in his ministry. In that case, although he may not have been clumsy in his editing, the evangelist certainly was heavy-handed in justifying the march of the Christian mission into the gentile world at the expense of the Jews. Seeking to deal with the problem of Luke 4 according to Conzelmann's schema, Hugh Anderson ponders its implications in exactly these terms:

> Does Luke wish to show that what is involved is just as much Jesus' rejection of the people as their rejection of him? At any rate, Jesus passes on directly to the parable of Elijah's and Elisha's ministering to the foreigners. And what appears to be signified for us *in advance* (for in Luke's gospel Jesus himself does not go to the Gentiles) is the final Jewish rejection of the fulfillment of Judaism in Jesus Christ and the turning of the gospel toward the Gentiles.[2]

Anderson is, of course, sharply aware of the material limitations of a redactional approach to this passage. The general assumption of Luke's literary dependence upon Mark rests very gingerly upon the meager verbal correspondence and disparate sequence that exist here between Mark and Luke. The lack of close parallels certainly cautions against describing Luke's account in terms of the "modification" of his Markan source.

Furthermore, even the content and theological substance of Luke's account appears to have been diminished or misconstrued by being viewed in contrast to Mark. To be sure, Luke does offer a public disclosure of the anointed Jesus with none able to gainsay his reign "today," and the power and glory of that inaugural display are the more clearly seen by contrast with Mark's account of Jesus' inability to perform miracles in the face of unbelief (Mark 6:6). Nevertheless, the matter of the reception of this disclosure is not simple in Luke's account. This is also a story of the intense interest, hope, wonder, doubt, rejection, and passionate rage of the people. It is a matter of "hearing and not hearing" the true prophet or executing the false prophet. There has been a shift in eschatological perspective from Mark's, and the "messianic secret" has not been kept. But the matter of response, the problem of the people's faith or unfaith, the question of the human situation in the light of divine disclosure have been raised much more comprehensively in Luke. Judging Luke as an alteration of Mark's eschatology or as a historicizing of his kerygmatic Christology, therefore, does not do justice to the theological or soteriological concern of his narrative.

Every description, of course, must be offered from some vantage point and on the basis of comparisons, and the strength of the "salvation history" interpretation of Luke–Acts arises largely from the *accuracy* which it derives from the comparison with Mark. But the question of the *adequacy* of that description to the material being interpreted has been raised by appealing to other perspectives on Luke–Acts. Thus, in a perceptive critique of Conzelmann's view of Luke's eschatological schema, Paul Minear remarked: "It is not too much to say that three temporal phrases or words in Luke 16:16, 4:21 and 22:36 are for him much more influential than the whole of chapters 1 and 2."[3]

In turn, it is not too much to say that subsequent work on Luke–Acts has confirmed the wisdom of Minear's appeal for more attention both to the scriptural substructure of the entire work and to its literary integrity, with particular attention to Luke 1–2 as an extended prologue Thus, Luke's view of the problem of the faithfulness of God to his scriptural promises to Israel looms in much sharper relief when compared to other contemporary Jewish expositions of those scriptures. And when Luke 4:16–30 is viewed as part of a literary composition, the evangelist's distinctive preoccupation with the effects of divine revelation on human observers and auditors may be followed from the prologue into this story.

Consequently, a brief analysis of Luke's extended prologue appears to commend itself as a promising avenue of approach to the programmatic text of Luke 4. Perhaps Jesus' sharp rejoinders and the intense rejection of his prophetic message are not so abrupt and unanticipated as they may appear in comparison with Mark. Perhaps the literary and hermeneutical agenda of the evangelist can be described more adequately by attending to his prologue to this encounter.

"That the Thoughts of Many Hearts May Be Revealed!"

The reclamation of the birth narratives and the recognition of the complementary continuity between John the Baptizer and Jesus are already indications of a new phase in studies of Luke–Acts. The very "Jewishness," archaic scriptural style, and heaping up of royal, prophetic, and priestly titles within these chapters can no longer be treated simply as due to more "primitive" semitic sources that have been introduced into this "gentile" Gospel. Not that the question of possible written or oral sources has been finally resolved. Indeed, the distinction between what most scholars now regard as an imitative Septuagintal style and a translation Greek that still displays semitic idioms will probably remain too fine to draw in most cases. Nevertheless, the evangelist's own hand is much more consistently perceived both in the careful structuring of the chapters and in the composition of individual episodes. Luke himself is to be credited with the neatly balanced diptych of annunciation and birth stories for John and Jesus with their concluding "growth refrains" echoing the scriptural stories of the childhood of the miraculously born prophet Samuel (Luke 1:80; 2:40,52; 1 Sam. 2:26; 3:19–20).[4]

The material in these chapters is condensed and cryptic, full of

23

ecstatic pronouncements, angelic oracles, and marvelous signs and portents. It is apparent that Luke was at home in a world where the legendary accounts of births of powerful kings, generals, and "benefactors" of humanity documented the early manifestations of divine providence in the subject's life. Perhaps the narrative itself only begins with the synchronism at 3:1, while chapters 1 and 2 constitute an extended prologue or preface, an overture to the larger work in which the critical themes are sounded. The overwhelming impression of Luke 1–2, which persists through chapter 3, however, is that Israel received this revealed messiah and savior in faith. With the literary device of a series of compact questions and comments of fearful wonder by the human participants, the evangelist has given glimpses of Israel's faithful response to these dramatic disclosures. Furthermore, in accord with his broad range of scriptural allusions, Luke emphasizes that the reception of such divine disclosures and pronouncements is a matter of the heart that is expectant and hopeful of the salvation of God. And he is prompt to display the contrast between disbelief and its consequences and obedient faith.

Only Zechariah, the first to hear of a miraculous birth signaling the Holy Spirit's renewal of Elijah's mission to "Turn the hearts of fathers to their children" (see Mal. 4:6; LXX 3:23, Sirach 48:10b), doubts. His disbelief is disclosed by means of his simple question, "How shall I know this?" apparently seeking some corroborating sign in the face of such incredible personal circumstances (1:18). Yet he is immediately punished by the messenger with muteness because[5] he "did not believe my words, which will be fulfilled in their time" (1:20).

All other human questions and responses of amazement in these chapters indicate faith and obedience. Mary's inquiry, "How can this be, since I have no husband?" is only a sign of wonder as her further comment reveals: "let it be to me according to your word" (1:34,38). Elizabeth's question is again one of simple faith: "Blessed are you among women . . . and why is this granted me that the mother of my Lord should come to me?" The fear and wonder of the friends and neighbors of Elizabeth and Zechariah who discussed these matters and "laid them up in their hearts" also prompt an expectant question, anticipating the manifestation of the prophet to Israel, "What then will this child be?" (1:66,80). And Zechariah's inspired prophetic canticle answers the question in powerful scriptural terms. Even the response of the multitudes to John's fiery preaching displays the faith of "all the people" (3:21). The "multitudes" asked "What then shall we do?" (3:10), as did also the tax collectors and soldiers in turn (3:12,14). When "the people were in expectation, and all men questioned in their hearts concerning John, whether perhaps he were the Christ" (3:15), Herod's evil act of imprisoning John appears quite arbitrary and unanticipated by any other opposition in Luke's account.[6]

Right up to John's imprisonment, these opening chapters of Luke are permeated with eager anticipation and faithful expectation. Everything is fulfilled in due time. The people "in expectation concerning John" might need correction concerning his role in the drama (3:15–17), but the question in their hearts is that of faith. So also, the people who await Zechariah's emergence from the temple (1:21: *prosdokan*), marveling at the delay, are able to recognize that he had seen a vision. Perhaps they are to be seen as part of that number at the temple of "all who were looking for the redemption of Jerusalem" (2:38: *prosdechesthai*). The shepherds make known what they had heard and glorify God for what they had "heard and seen" (2:15–20), and "Mary kept all these things, pondering them in her heart" (2:19).

The prologue sets the stage for faithful acceptance. The hearts of the people are open. Even Zechariah's initial lack of faith is transformed into ecstatic prophecy. Carried along by visions, prophetic oracles, and angelic visitations, and glowing with the cultivated memory of the faith of a "people prepared" (1:17; 7:27; Mal. 3:1), these chapters dwell on the glorious disclosure of divine fulfillment of prophecies and expectations. In fact, these chapters are so thoroughly permeated with the words of the ancient prophecies that they suggest a close community setting where a kind of archaic scriptural rhetoric is the living language of faith. Nevertheless, Luke portrays the drama of divine revelation and human reception against the broad background of the history of the Caesars, tetrarchs, governors, and high priests (3:1–2,18–20). In spite of the intra-Jewish cultural setting that is implied, the evangelist is already concerned to emphasize that "this was not done in a corner" (see Acts 26:26).

The fitting capstone to this carefully scripted and constructed account of divine disclosure and faithful response is Simeon's hymn of praise to God, the *nunc dimittis* treasured by the church. It states explicitly that what has now been seen and heard in this child with the eyes of faith is the salvation that God has "prepared before the face of all peoples, a light for disclosure to the Gentiles, and for the glory of your people Israel" (2:31–32, author's translation). Again, this story is not predisposed to judge the people as "slow of heart to believe all that the prophets have spoken" (24:25) or to suggest that "this people's heart has grown dull, and their ears are heavy of hearing, and their eyes they have closed" (Acts 28:27; Isa. 6:9–10). Faith has been found in Israel. Simeon's song testifies that God's plan of salvation for both Israel and the nations has been made manifest. It will not fail, and it will redound to Israel's glory. In fact, "only through the mediation of Israel is salvation also made available to the Gentiles."[7] As displayed in this child, the continuity of divine salvation is assured.

Yet the glory and triumph and the confidence which Simeon expresses toward God stand in sharp contrast to his second oracle of blessing to Mary. In phrases that ring with prophetic precedent (see especially Isa. 8:14–15,28) wherein God's plan of saving action also entails destruction for those who are found to oppose it, Simeon's word is strictly prophetic in this context. It is the first hint of future opposition. Thus, in spite of his ecstatic confidence in God's faithfulness to his promises and purposes, for Israel and the Gentiles, Simeon is presented as sharing the dark vision of Isaiah concerning the agony which this child portends for Israel, as well as the glory.

The oracle is crucial to the interpretation of Luke–Acts and to identifying how these prefatory chapters function to gather up the prophetic promises and anticipate the complex development of the narrative. Not every detail may be clear in such cryptic statements even in retrospect,[8] but the conflict between the declared divine purpose and the "many in Israel" is clearly foreshadowed. The concern of the rejection of the prophet, of the fate of the city, of the death of the messiah, and of the antipathy of "many in Israel" to Christian preaching is already set in sharp contrast to the praise of the faithful God.[9]

The question of the "predictability" of this rejection or its inevitability or necessity must be raised at this point, although it is too soon to attempt to describe in detail how such concepts function throughout Luke–Acts.[10] In the hellenistic world, such stories of the cryptic disclosure of the destiny of a gifted child by an ancient seer or oracle no doubt often evoked associations of determinism and fatalism, particularly when associated with heavenly signs and ancient prophecies.[11] Thus, when Simeon warns Mary that the infant "is set" for the fall and rising of many in Israel and the precocious Jesus rebukes her for not "knowing" that he "must be in my Father's house," (Luke 2:49) the matter of the character and content of this "necessity" is raised, but not yet defined.

Several scholars have argued persuasively that Luke's development of the concept of necessity is more properly interpreted against the backdrop of Jewish prophetic tradition than in reference to a Greek view of necessity wherein even the gods may be subject to the determined fates and forces that rule the cosmos.[12] Luke's own persistent use of those prophetic and deuteronomistic–historical texts certainly documents the vitality of such scriptural stories of Yahweh's direct involvement with his people, his indeflectable will to redeem, and the intensity and pathos of his wrath and mercy in relating to a willful people. The scriptures which were composed in the wake of the first destruction, with their painful questioning of responsibility for evil, the faithfulness of God, and the obedience of Israel were indeed the grist for Luke's mill.

Nevertheless, in the era of the second Jewish temple and its destruction, those Jewish traditions were interpreted with many of the same questions as were being addressed to classical Greek stories, histories, philosophies, and drama. Whether it was now the "tragic" or "pathetic" histories of the rhetorical style of Isocrates, the archaic imitators of Thucydides, or the philosophical schools and sects quarreling over the limits of human freedom and the measure of moral responsibility in the face of apparently arbitrary fates of empires and peoples, the problem of human freedom and determinism was common. Furthermore, the cosmopolitan circles of Jewish wisdom tradition which both gathered up those prophetic and deuteronomistic scriptural traditions and addressed them with a relatively elevated view of human responsibility had already mediated broader cultural views to Jewish considerations of the situation.[13] Among both Jews and Greeks, the spectrum of opinion on human freedom ranged from a rigid determinism with a mechanistic or apocalyptic view of the succession of empires in history to the ideal of the freedom of the truly wise man, whose freedom, however, arises from his knowledge of the truth and/or his knowledge of and obedience to the will of God.[14] The traditional Jewish concept of God as closely related to a particular people with a covenant of law and kingship certainly tempered any purely noetic views of freedom or abstract concepts of arbitrary fates and forces with an awareness of obedience to the word and will of God. But the distinction between what is Greek and what is Jewish again seems to promise more than it can deliver.

Consider Josephus's famous attempt to correlate the Jewish sects with Greek philosophical schools by comparing their concepts of the role of fate (*heimarmenē*) in human affairs:

> The Pharisees say that certain events are the work of Fate, but not all; as to other events, it depends upon ourselves whether they shall take place or not. The sect of the Essenes, however, declares that Fate is the mistress of all things, and that nothing befalls men unless it be in accordance with her decree. But the Sadducees do away with Fate, holding that there is no such thing . . . so that we are responsible for our own well-being.[15]

Josephus's typology may be far too neat, and its main value may be to serve only as a caution against hasty labels. The first task is rather a thorough description of how a particular text or tradition appropriates the deterministic language of Jewish and Greek traditions to interpret community experience.[16] Yet Josephus's correlation at least makes the commonality of the problem of human freedom and responsibility among Jews and Greeks inescapable.

Luke's presentation of the birth stories also testifies to divine activity in human affairs according to a predetermined plan. The vocabulary of "necessity" that is introduced here and rehearsed throughout Luke–Acts certainly would have evoked associations with the broad range of deterministic schemes and views of historical causation among contemporary philosophical schools and traditions of historiography. But Luke's use of this language constitutes a comment on or a contribution to that discussion from a particular viewpoint. The imitation of the scriptural tone of the deuteronomistic historians already recalls a theological tradition in which the determination or intention of God for his people sets the framework for discussing human freedom and responsibility. As a hellenistic historian, Luke both contemplates the inscrutable forces and causes of the fortunes of this people and draws upon archaic traditions to do so. But in concert with those prophetic and deuteronomistic scriptures upon which he draws, no mechanistic determinism or preordained sequence of inevitable events is allowed to eliminate actual human agency in its responsibility and limited freedom to affect the course of events. Finally, the flow of history is charted and "determined" by the interaction of God's fixed saving purpose for and covenants with his people and their actual obedience or resistance to God's dominion.

Even in Simeon's brief oracle, it is quite clear that there are no fates or forces above God which have "prepared" this salvation. Nor does this pronouncement envision a cosmic struggle against "principalities, against the powers, against the world rulers of this present darkness, against the spiritual hosts of wickedness in the heavenly places" (Eph. 6:12).[17] Rather this salvation has been disclosed within the history of Israel and displayed as "prepared in the presence of all peoples" (Luke 2:31). The passage is marked by its peculiar usage of the passive voice, "this child is set [keitai] for the fall and rising of many in Israel and for a sign spoken against . . . in order that the thoughts out of many hearts may be disclosed" (apokaluphthōsin, author's translation). But when preceded by Simeon's doxology for divine salvation, the initiating agency in these passives is not impersonal or even ambiguous. God is the agent indirectly adduced. Only the matter of how God will effect this salvation in the prospect of the predictable, indeed inevitable, human resistance remains obscure. The deploying of the reign of God within human history is the subject of this narrative, and the disclosure of the condition of the human heart is its concomitant purpose (see 2:35, *hopōs* plus the infinitive).

Luke has no easy optimism concerning human will and freedom. He might not be apt to say concerning every human that "every imagination of the thoughts of [his] heart was only evil continually" (Gen. 6:5), since at least the "pondering" in the hearts of Mary and the followers of John is disclosed as faithful (1:29; 3:15). But the dominant usage of the terms *dialogismos, dialogizesthai, dianoia,* and *dianoēma* points toward human suspicion (5:21–22; 11:17), hostile intentions (6:8; 20:14), self-delusions (1:51; 9:46–47; 12:17), and doubt (24:38). Thus, in the midst of the dramatic revelations of divine purpose and displays of faithfulness in these opening chapters, this cryptic oracle concerning the disclosing of the thoughts and schemes of the hearts of many forebodes resistance and rejection. A conflict of wills with at least a large part of Israel is anticipated, and apparently no middle ground will remain between acceptance and rejection, obedience and disobedience, falling and rising. The exposure of human hostility to the divine purpose and plan by this sign "spoken against" (see 2:12; 11:29) is a fundamental and predicted consequence of the disclosure of divine purposes.

It is critical to this study to observe that in his presentation of Jesus' ministry, death, and exaltation the evangelist has drawn upon an extensive and readily available pool of authoritative scriptural, particularly prophetic–deuteronomistic, traditions in which God's election of Israel was already the subject of thorough discussion. Through whatever specific channels of interpretation Luke's distinctive grasp of those scriptures may have developed,[18] the compelling and confounding mission of the prophet to reveal the purposes of the electing God and to display or even to cause the obduracy of the people had long been understood as basic to interpreting subsequent events in the prophet's career.[19] Furthermore, in Peter's sermon in Acts 3 (vv. 22–26), Luke explicitly identified Jesus as the "prophet like Moses" promised in Deuteronomy and rehearsed the command to "hear him in whatever he tells you" along with the attendant warning that "everyone who does not listen to that prophet shall be destroyed from the people."[20]

Thus Luke's appropriation of scriptural traditions in Simeon's oracle also reflects a highly specific view of the salvation of God (see Isa. 40:5, LXX), which this prophet-messiah Jesus portends for Israel, a view that was clearly subject to dispute. Indeed, the allusion to Isa. 49:6, enriched with words and phrases drawn from the larger context of those distinctive latter chapters of Isaiah, might well be regarded as a thematic statement of Luke's entire narrative: the call of the servant (*pais*) to restore the diaspora of Israel and to be a light to the Gentiles to the end of the earth. Not only is this fundamental to Luke's view of the death of the chosen servant-messiah (see explicitly Luke 22:37; Acts 8:32), but the rejection of this servant-messiah is also closely correlated to the offense of the inclusion of the Gentiles as Gentiles in the divine plan of salvation.

The volumes which have been written concerning the purpose of Luke–Acts with particular attention to the historiographical style of the formalized preface (1:1–4) may only demonstrate conclusively that the complexity of this work resists oversimplified explanations.[21] But from the vantage point of the materials considered in this study, the historiographical framework is also a crucial mark of Luke's hermeneutic of the fulfillment of the scriptures. Prophecy and human history are intertwined. History is not the story of humanity's submission to arbitrary fates and faceless fortunes or of the tragic plight of man seeking to live with character under the dominion of relentless powers. Rather, humanity is dealing and contending with a God who has elected to be involved with a people, a God whose will to shape history according to justice is tempered by a divine pathos and compassion for this people. What Abraham Heschel says of the prophets also sets the tone for Luke: "The central message of the prophets is the insistence that *the human situation can be understood only in conjunction with the divine situation.* . . . History is where God is defied, where His judgment is enacted, and where His kingship is to be established." Therefore, "the opposite of freedom is not determinism, but hardness of heart. Freedom presupposes openness of heart, of mind, of eye and ear" (emphasis in the original).[22]

Like the prophets in whose words his narrative is immersed, Luke testified both to the clarity of the disclosure of the divine plan in Jesus according to scriptural warrants and to the ambiguity with

31

which the human mind, heart, eye, and ear perceive that revelation. And even that human ambivalence is interpreted in scriptural terms. Simeon's two-edged oracles signal the juxtaposition of revelation and rejection that will characterize the narrative and affect the course of the story. In one sense, all that happens is the predetermined fulfillment of the scriptural plan of God, even the rejection, since like the prophets Luke is confident of the constancy and foreknowledge of God (see especially Acts 2:23; 3:18; 4:27–28; 13:29–33; 22:14; and Isa. 14:24–27; 6:9–13). Nevertheless, "the way in which the Lord carries out His plan remains inscrutable. But He employs human agents as well as 'a sword not of man' to accomplish His designs."[23] The specific course of the narrative is therefore shaped and determined by the interaction between God's purpose in Jesus and actual human response. But the scriptures and their fulfillment are thus the crucial testimony to the constancy and indeflectability of the divine will in retrospect and prospect of its apparent frustration in the refusal of the messiah and the tragic fate of the nation. Confidence in God and in the reign of the messiah Jesus was still vulnerable to the burden of such apparently unfulfilled promises.

The evangelist maintained that not even the faithful could always understand what Jesus was about. His parents "did not understand" his word concerning what it was necessary for him to do (2:49–50). His disciples "understood none of these things" with respect to his third passion prediction for "this saying was hid from them, and they did not grasp what was said" (18:34). Even after the risen Jesus has opened their minds to understand (24), at the time of the ascension, the disciples are again explicitly warned that "it is not for you to know times or seasons which the Father has fixed by his own authority" (Acts 1:7). But such lack of understanding or "ignorance of the faithful" is specific to Luke's account and can be distinguished from both the ignorance of the messianic secret which leads to misunderstanding and betrayal in Mark and from the tragic and culpable ignorance of Israel for not knowing "the time of your visitation" (Luke 19:41–44; see chapter 3 below). Indeed the "ignorance of the faithful" can be identified as a literary technique for alerting the reader that as the narrative unfolds, the divine plan will be disclosed in greater detail. But it also serves to alert the interpreter that while history testifies to God's continuing saving activity, even the faithful will not always be able to explain or schematize the means or phasing of that salvation.

Perhaps no New Testament author is more concerned than Luke to testify to the accomplishment of the will of God in history or so caught up in the language of the divine plan and predetermined intention, purpose, and necessity. Furthermore, Luke–Acts is framed with oracles and speeches concerned with demonstrating the case that the death of the messiah and the inclusion of the Gentiles were warranted by the scriptures as consistent with the divine plan, thereby also demonstrating that this case was far from self-evident (see especially Acts 26:22–23; 28:23–30). The conviction that the Christian community could be identified with a reconstituted faithful Israel whose mission among Gentiles redounded to the glory of Israel was vulnerable to attacks from without and dispute from within. Especially when Jerusalem lay in ruins, such theological affirmations and hermeneutical arguments would have been filled with a new passion. The literary balance and contrast of Simeon's two-edged oracles must, therefore, be acknowledged as expressing the hope and reflecting the anguish of the community. The child Jesus, who evokes doxology toward God from the faithful who have looked for the fulfillment of the saving promises for Israel and the Gentiles, will also prove to be a source of scandal and division.

"Is Not This Joseph's Son?"

Approaching Luke 4:14–30 from the perspective developed above requires at least a brief word concerning the intervening baptism and temptation stories. Neglecting them could create the false impression that Luke presented the story of Jesus as mere human history. But whatever else his silence about John's role in the baptism may mean, Luke clearly was intent on stressing the direct agency of the Holy Spirit in this "anointing" (see Acts 10:38–39). His tracing of Jesus' genealogy all the way back to Adam, "the son of God" (3:38) was similarly distinctive. Luke's repetitive phrasing that Jesus, returning "full of the Holy Spirit," was led "by the Spirit" in the wilderness makes obvious his emphasis upon divine participation and contention with larger than human forces and power. In his narrative, there is no rigid dichotomy between human and superhuman agencies.

The peculiar conclusion to Luke's account of the "temptation" story also calls for brief comment. Not only does the sequence of the episodes, now ending in the temple, seem to correspond neatly with his special interests in the connection between Jesus and the temple,[24] but Luke's distinctive conclusion has also been seen to fit with his eschatological schema. The completion of "every temptation" and departure of the devil "until the opportune time" (4:13) has been said to inaugurate a "Satan-free period" in the middle of time, during which the reign of God is freely deployed.[25] Certainly the exorcism stories and the sending out of the twelve and the seventy to cast out demons should caution against an overstatement of this interpretation. Perhaps that concluding statement should be regarded simply as another sign of literary skill, creating anticipation for the crucial moment in the narrative when Satan "returns" in league with Judas and the chief priests and captains to betray Jesus (22:3). Nevertheless, it does appear consistent with Luke's interests to suggest that having shown him to be more than a match for the devil and his minions, the evangelist next introduced Jesus "in the power of the Spirit" to the arena of human affairs in Galilee.

Here the struggle is more complex. Here the anointed "Son of God" who had been acclaimed by the heavenly voice (3:22) and proved by the trials of the devil (4:3,9) was now to be disclosed as the prophet anointed by the Spirit to address Israel. But in that role and arena, genuine conflict and opposition were also destined to emerge. The fate of the prophet and the people were intertwined, and the specter of rejection hangs over him and them. Invincible with respect to the cosmic powers of evil and, for the moment, immune from human attempts on his life, Jesus would "at the opportune time" prove vulnerable when such adversaries would act in collusion with Satan. Yet what would that bode for them?

The story of Jesus in Nazareth is a tale well told. Its literary structure and features show that it is carefully calculated to draw the reader into the confounding drama of the disclosure of the salvation of God in the person and message of the prophet while human disdain for that revelation is also made manifest. The passage falls into two obvious segments, Jesus' programmatic announcement and the ensuing harsh conflict with the crowd. Each segment features the direct appropriation of scriptural prophetic traditions and their application to the moment. And between them, in perhaps a single verse (4:22), the matter appears to hang in the balance, with only a question tipping the scales, alerting the reader to what is going on in the hearts of the crowd and anticipating the conclusion of the episode: "Is not this Joseph's son?"

Like the two-volume work as a whole,[26] the passage sustains highly detailed assessments of its construction, perhaps providing one of the more convincing New Testament examples of chiastic literary structure. The first segment leading up to Jesus' one-sentence pronouncement lends itself admirably to a diagram that displays a series of consecutive clauses leading into and out of the Isaiah text with strikingly repetitive procedural detail:

> *And* he came to Nazareth, where he had been brought up
>
> A.   *And* he entered as his custom was on the sabbath day into the *synagogue*
>
> B.   *And stood up* to read
>
> C.   *And* there *was given to him* the book of the prophet Isaiah
>
> D.   *And* when he *opened the book* he found the place where it was written
>
> E.   "The Spirit of *the Lord* is upon me, Because he has anointed me to *preach good news* to the poor
>
> F.   He has sent me to proclaim *release* to the *captives*
>
> G.   And recovering of sight to the blind,
>
> F.′   [To send forth the *oppressed* in *release*]
>
> E.′   To *proclaim* the *acceptable year* of the *Lord*
>
> D.′   *And* when he had *closed the book*
>
> C.′   Having *given it back* to the attendant
>
> B.′   He *sat down*
>
> A.′   *And* the eyes of all in the *synagogue* were fixed on him.[27]

It has even been suggested that the phrase from Isa. 58:6 (F.′) was substituted for the words of Isa. 61:1 ("to heal those afflicted of heart") in order to keep the parallelism intact.[28] But such a tidy solution to the complex problem of Luke's interpretive usage of scriptural material should not be adopted too hastily, nor should it be taken for granted that the Isaiah text which was being used must have agreed with those Greek and Hebrew texts of Isaiah that are now available.

Nevertheless, the story displays careful composition. Even diligent efforts to get behind the text to what Jesus himself had in mind in, Nazareth must credit the evangelist with preserving or creating the lively realism and suspense of the story. First Luke relates the elaborate ritual of coming, entering, standing, receiving, unrolling, finding, and then closing, returning, and sitting. Also, his word for the observers' "fixing the eyes" suggests the watchers' intense regard without displaying commitment.[29] After Jesus' pronouncement that "Today this scripture has been fulfilled in your hearing," the question of what they have actually "heard" is unresolved. Luke supplies three verbs in the imperfect tense, conveying a sense of a somewhat prolonged process of "witnessing," "wondering," and "speaking." All of these terms are potentially positive, yet ambiguously neutral in the context. Only the qualification that the words from his mouth were judged "gracious" indicates clear approbation, but considering how few and cryptic were Jesus' own words, the "gracious words" may merely suggest clear approval for the glorious phrases of Isaiah. Furthermore, in the light of the stunning claim and announcement implicit in Jesus' terse exposition, the response of the people seems banal, even if it is generally pleasant.[30]

But when their discussion comes to the point where they are *asking* "Is not this Joseph's son?" Luke's Jesus turns his prophetic announcement into an equally prophetic indictment. And even before the scriptural content of the statements has been assessed, the formal or literary structure of the passage quickly displays the gathering of diverse materials, almost like a statement of charges.[31]

The opening phrase is predictive, prefaced by an emphatic adverb (*pantōs ereite moi*: "certainly you will say to me"). That remark governs the entire sentence that follows and sharpens the directness with which Jesus charges the crowd with yet unstated objections. The construction has the additional literary function of anticipating Jesus' statements of rebuttal, which are also prefaced with emphatic adverbs (*amēn legō humin, ep' alētheias de legō humin*, "Truly I say to you," vv. 24,25). The shift in persons bringing charges is also carefully balanced: "You will say to me," "but I say to you." One old maxim about the "physician" evokes another concerning the "prophet" and the question of how Jesus would relate to his homeland is answered in terms of prophetic precedent. Furthermore, the vocabulary of Luke's distinctive version of the proverb about the prophet not only links it to the immediate context concerning homeland (*patris*, vv. 23,24) but also back to the groundwork of the story in the Isaiah text: the anointed prophet who proclaims the *acceptable* year of the Lord is not *acceptable* in his homeland.

In its larger context, this prediction of rejection probably anticipates that after Jesus has been in Capernaum where faith will be found (Luke 4:31–43), these people will insist on his also demonstrating his powers among his own. Or perhaps it is to be taken in the light of previous acts in Capernaum only alluded to in the summary in 4:14–15. In any case, Jesus ascribes the objections to them in advance. Thus, the passage turns sharply on the unadorned question about Jesus' parentage, with all that follows serving to explicate its implications. In a tour de force that is reminiscent of scriptural passages wherein Yahweh confronts those who would accuse or question him, Jesus appears to expose or perhaps stimulate violent opposition.[32]

The conclusion consists of one complex sentence (vv. 28–29) in which the rage, rejection, and intention of the people to kill Jesus are displayed directly along with a brief statement, without explanation, that Jesus went his way by passing through their midst (v. 30). In its cryptic way, this sentence does complete the episode; yet it offers only what has come before to interpret the wrath with which "they were filled," and it leaves the reader pondering what dire fate awaits Jesus as he proceeds on his way.[33]

Considerable literary skill can thus be noted in the way the evangelist has heightened the tension between Jesus and the people within the episode and alerted the reader to expect more of the same as the narrative continues. Furthermore, the literary techniques employed point up the concern which the text seeks to interpret. That is, in the context of treating a highly elaborate combination of royal and prophetic functions and titles, the reader is not so much led to ponder "Who is this Jesus?" in quest of a correct Christology as to wonder

"What is going on between Jesus and the people?" In contrast, Mark's account (6:1–6a) suggests that the matter of Jesus' family was directly offensive and the accompanying references to Mary may constitute further aspersions on his paternity. For Mark, the content of the people's unbelief *is* christological, and even Jesus appears incapacitated and awed by such unbelief.

To be sure, Luke would also regard the question of the people, "Is not this Joseph's son?" as woefully inadequate and in error christologically. Luke has, of course, also identified Joseph as Jesus' father in previous contexts (see Luke 2:33,41,42,48),[34] so the content of the question is not automatically judged as vicious. But the reader who has followed Jesus through his virginal conception and childhood, anointing in baptism, and testing by the devil knows that this "son of Joseph" is truly the "son of God" (see especially 2:48–50), appointed to inaugurate God's reign. In Luke, Jesus' identity has been clearly displayed. The mystery which requires interpretation is that of the people's rejection.

The fury they unleash on Jesus is not simply a christological error or misunderstanding. As Luke's use of strategic questions in the prologue has shown, the primary literary function of their question is to disclose their own stance toward the message that is being delivered. But in the light of Jesus' previous dramatic pronouncement, their question displays a singularly inappropriate *ad hominem* response. Perhaps the emphatic use of the demonstrative pronoun (*houtos*) even suggests a sharp edge to their question (see 5:21; 23:38; Acts 6:14), but the content of their refusal to listen is not explicated. By ascribing this question to them, Luke has depicted them as refusing to listen out of hand, using the question to evade the message, as if choosing to remain ignorant of the reign of God that has been announced so forthrightly.

In order to explore Luke's grasp of this refusal more thoroughly, repeated references to the mission speeches to Israel in Acts will need to be made (see 2:14–42; 3:12–26; 7:2–53; 13:16–41; 28:23–29).[35] But for the moment, two observations must suffice. First, even a brief check of those passages guards against the trivializing of the "ignorance" concerning Jesus which a literary analysis exposes so badly.

In one sense, this "ignorance" is viewed as the cause of the rejection, almost as if to explain or excuse such refusals as that in the Nazareth story (Acts 3:17; 13:27); but this is not really the case. Jesus had been attested by God to the "men of Israel . . . as you yourselves know" (Acts 2:22). The culpability for this ignorance is sharply defined in Acts as also representing the ignorance of "the utterances of the prophets which are read every sabbath" in the synagogue (Acts 13:27; 3:18: "all the prophets"; 10:42–43).[36] Yet in another sense, the mystery of the place of this ignorance and refusal to listen in the divine plan of salvation persists to the end of Acts, since in chorus with Isaiah 6 Luke ascribes even this unwillingness and inability to understand to God's long-standing intention. Second, as the last comment indicates, literary analysis may be adequate to help identify crucial turning points in the narrative and the internal coherence of the work, but further assessments of Luke's hermeneutical agenda and methods will also be required to explicate the content of such formal observations. And there is probably no better illustration of this than the refusal of Luke 4.

"Today, This Scripture Has Been Fulfilled in Your Hearing!"

The scriptural resources which have been directly adduced or even cited in Luke 4:16–30 are so formidable as to discourage further searching for subtle allusions or implicit references. With the possible exception of Matthew's formula quotations taken together, no other portion of the New Testament provides such a compact, thorough and explicit example of early Christian hermeneutics. Furthermore, the text of Isaiah 61, as enriched with an allusion to Isaiah 58, is set in juxtaposition with references to stories in 1 and 2 Kings. Thus, Luke has provided an admirable illustration of the contemporary Jewish practice of interpreting scriptural texts by means of other scriptural texts.

Nevertheless, before returning to a more detailed assessment of the way Luke appropriates texts from Isaiah and Kings, it is necessary to refer to two other scriptural traditions that are vital to Luke's understanding of Israel's complex role in the divine plan. Both are cited explicitly within the speeches to Israel in Acts and are clearly fundamental to the purposes of the evangelist in the work as a whole.

First, in citing and alluding to the promises of a "prophet like Moses" in Deuteronomy 18 and 34 (See Acts 3:22; 7:35–37), Luke was joining a long-standing and diverse hermeneutical discussion. The passages themselves clearly invited such discussion since they raised the prospect of a "prophet" successor to Moses while at the same time insisting that Moses' immediate successor Joshua (LXX: *Iēsous*) did not fill the bill. For although Joshua was "filled with the spirit of understanding since Moses had laid his hands upon him," still "there has not yet arisen [*anestē*] a prophet like Moses" (Deut. 34:9–10, author's translation). These passages which spoke of Moses as the "servant" of the Lord also constituted a fundamental contribution to the idea that Israel's salvation and election were assured and restored through the intercession and obedience of the servant-prophet, including his suffering the wrath of God on Israel's account (Deut. 3:23–28; 4:21–27). According to Deuteronomy, Israel's election was emphatically not due to the obedience and righteousness of the people, but was secured for them by the prophet who both accused the people of their sin and still carried their cause to God in a plea for divine compassion based upon faithfulness to ancient promises (see Deuteronomy 9). It is "because the Lord loves you, and is keeping the oath which he swore to your fathers" that "the Lord your God has chosen you to be a people for his own possession, out of all the peoples that are on the face of the earth" (Deut. 7:6–8.)[37]

The Deuteronomy 18 passage concerning the prophet like Moses also furnished the critical test for false prophecy, that is, when the word spoken in the name of the Lord "does not come to pass or come true, that is a word which the Lord has not spoken; the prophet has spoken it presumptuously [LXX: *en asebeia*], you need not be afraid of him" (see also 1 Kings 22:26–29; Jeremiah 28; Deut. 18:22). Deuteronomy 13 further established that the false prophet who leads the people into idolatory shall be put to death by stoning, even if he performs signs or wonders. The matter of Israel's "hearing" and fearing and faithfulness to the covenant of its election would thus be tested "to know what was in your heart" (Deut. 8:2).

Subsequent development and comment upon the concept of the suffering of the prophet must also be noted. Not only was such a motif versatile and adaptable for diverse applications, but the figure of Moses could also be invoked on behalf of contested claims concerning the identity of the faithful in Israel. Thanks to Deuteronomy, the suffering of the prophet functioned both to indict Israel of unfaithfulness and to offer assurance of divine faithfulness to the elect when in distress. While subject to immense alteration, these diverse appropriations of the Moses figure can be evaluated in terms of their places in a spectrum of views concerning the identity of the true Israel, frequently as reflected in their specific adaptations of the text of Deuteronomy.

In Sirach's "praise of famous men, and our fathers in their generations," for example, Moses the "man of mercy," "chosen out of all mankind," and "sanctified through faithfulness and meekness" (45: 1–5) stands forth as an exemplar of nobility. Again it is Moses, the "holy prophet," whose rejection and exposure by the Egyptians also was turned into the vindication of the righteous of Israel who is placarded in the Wisdom of Solomon (11). For Philo of Alexandria, Moses the prophet is primarily Moses the sage who manifests moral virtue. And the author of the Testament of Moses allows that Moses' prophecies entailed his having "suffered many things in Egypt and in the Red Sea" (3:12). But it is the suffering incurred at the hands of Israel that Deuteronomy highlights. And thus in Josephus, even the scriptural account of Moses' skepticism at divine promises (Num. 9:21–22) is transformed along these lines into an illustration of the solidarity of the suffering prophet with God before Israel: " 'God,' said he, 'and I, though vilified by you, will never cease our efforts on your behalf' " (*Antiq.* 3.298). So also in pseudo-Philo, the yearning for a successor to Moses yields a transparent allusion to the promises of Deuteronomy, now interpreted in terms of shepherd, judge, and intercessor: "Who will give us another sheperd like Moses, or such another judge to the children of Israel, to pray for our sins at all times, and to be heard for our iniquities?"[38]

The powerful appeal of Moses and his successor Joshua[39] can be described in much more detail to document how their distinctive traits were maximized in differing traditions. But even these passing references serve to emphasize that in his presentation of Jesus as the "prophet like Moses," Luke was entering a Jewish hermeneutical fray as well as probably rehearsing Jewish-Christian exegetical preaching traditions. In Acts 7, it is the *refusal* and thrusting aside (vv. 35,39) of the ruler-judge-redeemer who had led them out (*exagein*) with signs and wonders that is the focal point. In Acts 3:22–23, the penalty for not heeding the prophet like Moses is specified in terms that are much more forceful than in Deuteronomy. By "enriching" the allusion to Deuteronomy with Lev. 23:29, the consequence for not "hearing the prophet" is to be "destroyed from the people." Faithful Israel does hear (Deut. 18:15, *akouein*). Refusing to obey (*hupakouein*) is a sign that "in their hearts they turned to Egypt" and is tantamount to idolatry (Acts 7:39–43; see Deuteronomy 13).

A second complex of references and allusions in Luke concerning the reception and rejection of the prophet and his message to Israel indicates that the Isaiah traditions have been used to complement Deuteronomy's statements concerning the "hearing and not hearing" of Israel. Without appealing to the notion of a pre-Lucan book of "testimonies" or even assuming that the evangelist was consciously attempting to reconcile all of this material, it is clear that the explicit citations of Isaiah serve to specify Luke's interpretation of Israel's response.

Thus, in the speech to Israel at the unsettled ending of the book of Acts (28:25–28), the matter of "hearing and not hearing" is interpreted by direct reference to Isaiah's harsh vocation as a prophet (see also Luke 8:10). From Matthew 13:14–15 and John 12:40, it is also clear that this Isaiah passage was subject to wider usage among Christians to interpret the rejection of Jesus and Christian preaching by many Jews. The nonbiblical Jewish traditions that Isaiah was martyred by being sawn in two and that other prophets were similarly slaughtered also contributed to the view that the violent fate of the prophet was the predictable if not inevitable consequence of the burden of his message to a disobedient people.[40] Certainly the concept of the suffering prophet whose message exposes the sinful hearts of the people and precipitates his rejection or even death and whose intercession effects the gifts of repentance was not original with Luke or extraneous to Jewish tradition. Nevertheless, with the explicit addition of the Isaiah 6 text, Luke reproves obdurate Israel for not "hearing" . . . "Moses and the prophets" (Acts 28:33) and reinforces his presentation of the refusal of Moses as the prototype of the rejection and killing of the prophets.[41]

The citation of Isaiah 53 in the story of Philip and the Ethiopian must also be mentioned briefly in close connection with the scriptural traditions from Deuteronomy and Isaiah 6 concerning the obduracy of Israel and the suffering of the prophet. Because the assumption of a widespread pre-Christian doctrine of a "suffering servant" based on the songs in deutero-Isaiah has been successfully challenged,[42] the case for attributing interpretive activity to Luke's use of these traditions in his composition is in turn strengthened. Not only does Luke 22:37 contain the only explicit synoptic application of Isaiah 53 to the passion, but the question of the eunuch in Acts 8 once again serves as Luke's heuristic device. In asking, "About whom, pray, does the prophet say this, about himself or about someone else?" the concept of the suffering prophet is again established as the framework for telling "the good news of Jesus, . . . beginning with this scripture" (8:34–35).

On returning to the explicit use of scriptural traditions in Luke 4, it ought now be possible to demonstrate that the theological "content" of the passage is congruent with its literary form and redoubles its force while specifying its meaning. It is probably impossible to make an exact determination of degree to which the evangelist has assembled the collection of scriptures mentioned above by direct reference to the texts or has drawn them from a broad mixture of passages that had already proven crucial to Christian expositions concerning Jesus in the synagogues. Nor does this citation of diverse passages concerning the reception of the prophet do justice to the range of associations and implicit appeals they were used to evoke. Yet it may assist in the more exact recognition of the programmatic concerns which the passages from Isaiah 61 and Kings were to serve. For along with his literary skill in telling the story, Luke's appropriation of traditions concerning the rejected and suffering prophet probably also made his account into a pointed commentary on his own time.

The Isaiah 61 passage itself presents an intrascriptural midrash in which the one who proclaims the jubilee (Lev. 25:10) is apparently identified in terms of a prophetic figure strikingly reminiscent of the servant songs of 2 Isaiah.[43] The conviction that this prophet-herald is "anointed" by the Spirit not only to announce but to execute royal political functions already presents a remarkable coalescence of traditions. To be sure, 1 Kings 19:15–16 also speaks of the "anointment" of the prophet Elisha as successor by Elijah, and Sirach, which has many other similarities to Luke's presentation of the prophet Elijah, takes note of this anointing (48:8). Nevertheless, Isaiah 61 appears singularly appropriate for the formation and informing of Luke's concept of Jesus' role in Israel.

From the vantage point of modern critical scholarship on this section of Isaiah, it may be possible to describe something of the natural appeal and force of such a tradition. For if 2 Isaiah can be seen as taking up the election traditions of David and Zion and rehearsing them according to the dominant election traditions of the exodus, then Isaiah 61 appears as a poetic exposition of that rehearsal, with particular literary and theological affinities to the "servant songs."[44] Not that the evangelist or other early Christian expositors had any hint of such schematic labeling of the traditions, but here was a passage doing what they wanted to do and telling them how to do it. Here was a succinct restatement of election traditions in which the anointed prophet was both the herald and the agent of the reign of God. Here the prophetic bias for the poor and the role of Israel among all the nations were articulated. Here the glorious mission of the one upon whom the Spirit of the Lord comes with anointing was enunciated in phrases that also rang with the songs of the servant who suffers. To suggest either that the evangelist "selected" this text or that the text "wrote the program" for his narrative would, nevertheless, fall short of the mark. For not only is Isaiah 61 a mosaic of earlier election traditions, but Luke's reuse of it in order to authorize and define his presentation of Jesus displays the lively processes by which broader scriptural resources were again appropriated to interpret this "fulfillment." No static view of the text or its redaction will prove adequate to Luke's hermeneutic.

The royal messianic heritage of the city and lineage of David, the enthronement psalm (2) identifying Jesus as son of God or regent, and the testing of this son of God by the devil are all emphatic in Luke's understanding of the "Lord's Christ" (Luke 2:26). Similarly in Acts, the Davidic covenant is immediately adduced, although it is David the prophet (2:30) and servant (*pais*: see also Luke 1:69), speaking by the Holy Spirit (4:25) who testifies to this Lord, that is, Jesus, who is also the anointed of the Lord (2:36; 4:26).

Furthermore, beginning with the baptism wherein John the Baptizer is already out of the scene, Luke is at pains to describe Jesus' "anointing" in terms of the outpouring of the Spirit upon a prophet.[45] Jesus' being "full of the Holy Spirit" and returning "in the power of the Spirit" is the prelude to the Nazareth episode. Again, in Acts, the first passage concerning the prophet like Moses stands between the references to David just mentioned. And while the "anointed" David is identified as prophet and servant, Moses the prophet is shortly thereafter presented as ruler and deliverer (*archōn kai lutrōtēs*: 7:35). Given the frequent scriptural identification of Moses as "the servant of God," especially in contexts speaking of judgments on Israel's unfaithfulness, the absence of the expected parallel reference to Moses as *pais* is surprising. Nevertheless, the references to Jesus as *pais* stand in close correlation with both Moses (3:13,26) and David (4:27,30; see 4:25).

In spite of the persistent emphasis on divine initiative in these views of David and Moses, treating them as "election traditions" requires additional comment lest it appear to be a category only imposed on the texts. And it must be granted that the epithet "the servant of God" is so pervasive in the Jewish scriptures as to preclude its limitation to usage in service of a single theological agenda. Yet its peculiar cogency for articulating Israel's complex awareness of God's commitments to them made through his chosen agents was crucial to the extended discussion concerning Israel's election in the long years of the peril, destruction, and reconstruction of Jerusalem. The powerful assurance to Zion and Jerusalem that they were secure in their election because of God's promises to "my servant David, whom I have anointed with holy oil"[46] stand in juxtaposition to the deuteronomistic and prophetic critique of kingship (see especially Deut. 28; 17:14–20; and Jeremiah 32). The cultivation of the concept of the long-suffering Moses, prophet and servant of God, is further documentation of this synthesizing of election traditions which was still continuing in Luke's own day, stimulated afresh by the national crises of the war.[47]

Within specifically Christian tradition, as well, Luke was both an heir and an agent of this process. In all three synoptic versions, the voice from heaven at the baptism already suggests an "enriched" appropriation of the enthronement psalm with the vocabulary concerning the son/servant favored by God. But this is further explicated in Luke when the voice from the clouds speaks the second time: "This is my son, my chosen, hear him" (Luke 9:35, author's translation). Not only is the allusion to the chosen of God whom Israel must hear (see Isa. 42:1; 44:1) thus much more overt, but Luke fortifies the allusion by relating that Moses and Elijah had been speaking with Jesus concerning the "exodus" which he was about to "fulfill" in Jerusalem (Luke 9:28–36).[48] As a result, when Luke's Jesus is derided on the cross, it is the peculiar qualification of his being "the chosen one" that conveys Luke's views of this "anointed one" who is also titled "the king of the Jews" (23:35–38; see chapter 4 below).

Attempting to decide whether Jesus' "anointing" in Luke 4 is essentially royal-Davidic or prophetic-Mosaic proves, therefore, to be at least risky and probably futile. The degree to which these scriptural traditions, which now seem quite disparate in origin and function, were distinguished by the disciples of Isaiah or the evangelists can only be estimated with caution. In drawing upon a broad spectrum of scriptural resources, however, the evangelist has taken up election traditions associated with both of these "servants of God" along with assurances of God's choice of Zion and applied them in the service of a new discussion of the election of Israel. Nothing short of the testimony of all the prophets, the psalms, and Moses will be brought to bear in his presentation.

Yet Luke's appropriation of Isaiah 61 is marked most directly by the disjunction of rejection, displaying an acute awareness of a deep division within Israel and a sensitivity to the charge that the assurance offered by Jesus is itself a cause of offense. In that light, the precedent of conflict concerning true and false prophecy and the debate over the causes of Israel's peril preserved by the deuteronomist, Jeremiah, and their contemporaries is the more telling. Indeed, no great risk is involved in the interpretation of Luke 4 to suggest that it represents a Christian response to the charge that Jesus was a false prophet. The question of whether the people will hear or listen to what is spoken "in their ears" is clearly a question of Israel's faithfulness or obduracy, that is, as asked from the viewpoint of those who have already accepted Jesus as the prophet like Moses or the true prophet "who prophesies peace" as in Deuteronomy 18 and 34 and Jeremiah 28. It is crucial to note that those same traditions (see Deuteronomy 13 and Jer. 11:21) also require faithful Israel to refuse to listen to the false prophet and demand his death. Even the manner of execution by stoning probably corresponds to Luke's picture of their attempt on Jesus' life.[49] Yet such a matter is to be decided after deliberation and the verification or nonverification of the prophet's word, which Luke then provides quite explicitly for those who have "seen" and "heard" the fulfillment of the promises of Jesus' pronouncement (Luke 7:16,22–23). Thus, the narrative takes careful account of the dilemma posed by Israel's scriptural heritage in discerning the true prophet. But it portrays the rejection of Jesus as precipitous, indicting this initial response as faithless refusal to receive the "prophet whom I shall raise up from among their brothers . . . not giving heed to my words which he shall speak in my name" (Deut. 18:18–19, author's translation).

James A. Sanders has provided a particularly cogent reading of Luke 4 by means of "comparative midrash." Highlighting the contrast with the usage of Isaiah 61 in the exegesis of Qumran, Sanders has demonstrated that the hermeneutics ascribed to Jesus provoke the offense taken by the listeners in the story. On the one hand, the recitation of eschatological promises and the announcement of their fulfillment in the critical present would be met with acceptance or goodwill according to the canons of eschatological exegesis at Qumran (see IQS 18:14–15; pes. Ps. 37:11), and probably would have found an interested or perhaps even a favorable hearing in Nazareth. But "the specific application of the Isaiah passage" challenges the assumption that God's wrath is for the outsiders and his mercy is for the elect of Israel. The addition of the stories concerning Elijah and Elisha thus constitutes a "prophetic critique," a hermeneutical corrective characteristic of Jeremiah's challenges to the "official theology" of Israel's election in his day. It is the stance of one within Israel, yet one whose vision of God's grace and wrath so surpasses the bounds of the protection of parochial interests, even those of race, blood, soil, and cultus, that it sets the prophet at odds with his own people. Thus, finally, Luke's Jesus demonstrates the plight and tragedy of the prophet:

> No prophet, that is, no true prophet of the Elijah, Amos, Isaiah, Jeremiah type, is *dektos* by his own countrymen precisely because his message always must bear in it a divine challenge to Israel's covenantal self-understanding in any generation. In other words, a true prophet of the prophet-martyr tradition *cannot* be *dektos* at home precisely because of his hermeneutics.[50]

It is crucial to observe, however, that this "prophetic critique" can be defended as the evangelist's own perspective. That is, instead of regarding the evangelist as standing with Melito or Eusebius, who draw upon such prophetic critiques from Jeremiah and Jesus to justify a new elect—a gentile church as the expense of Israel—the case can now be made that the "today" of Jesus' sermon continues to lay down the prophetic gauntlet to any group claiming the promises of Israel.

The matter is fundamental to the interpretation of all of Luke–Acts and yet very difficult to determine with certainty. Ascribing genuine compassion for Israel to the evangelist might well have been viewed, until quite recently, with more suspicion than an effort to assign such hermeneutics to the historical Jesus himself. Sanders admits to "an innate reverse skepticism" about efforts to claim all originality in the name of the evangelists, and thus he appeals to the prophetic mode of the parables to ascribe this hermeneutic to Jesus.[51] And it must be granted that the criterion of dissimilarity has indeed been used too frequently to obliterate Jesus' own probable impact upon the gospel traditions. But the same complaint must be lodged against any assumption that the evangelist merely transmitted this stance or preserved and reinforced it only to vindicate the church over against "Israel." Even if the "critique" originated with Jesus, it can be shown to be vital to Luke's purposes that a new "elect" has not simply displaced the old and that the critical stance of Jesus, as opposed to those who were confident that God's wrath was for outsiders alone and his grace was for them, has not been domesticated by the evangelist. Here, above all, is where historical and introductory assumptions concerning the author's identity and place within or outside of the synagogue must be carefully examined.

The case is probably more complex than such sharp alternatives between "insiders" and "outsiders" would suggest. As has been noted, when the rhetoric about "the Jews" becomes increasingly polemical in the later chapters of Acts, it is clear that sectarian accusations were not beyond the author. But the extravagance and intensity of all prophetic indictments creates an unavoidable chasm between the prophet and the people, which may appear quite unbridgeable by any identification with "them." Consider Isaiah's prayer against Israel, "Forgive them not!" (2:9), or Jeremiah's words of judgment, "thus says the Lord God: Behold, my anger and my wrath will be poured out on this place, upon man and beast, upon the trees of the field and the fruit of the ground; it will burn and not be quenched" (7:20). Such oracles and caustic polemics are always vulnerable to misappropriation. Only an awareness of the pathos of the prophet, caught up in the sorrow and ardor and wrath of God dealing with his people, prevents vicious misuse of such passages for self-justification.

Since the mode of gospel narrative generally obscures the evangelist's own application of the material, it may be impossible to establish more than that the burden of proof should be shifted onto claims that Luke was justifying the gentile mission at the expense of Jewish rejection. That is, most commentators acknowledge the thematic development of Luke 4 in the rest of the work, but Luke's exploitation of the scriptural motifs of this passage enroute to the parting salvo of Acts 28 is generally described in terms of a salvation history for the church, which is but a thinly veiled damnation history for Israel. Yet it may be possible to challenge this view and suggest that, as presented by the evangelist, Jesus' critique of an exclusivist or self-justifying and constitutive understanding of Israel's election continues to wield a sharp edge of reproof in Luke's own view of the church as true Israel. What is crucial is the way these scriptural traditions function throughout the whole of the narrative to address and interpret a problem of continuing significance within Luke-Acts, that is, the gentile question.

It is necessary to state the matter sharply since this reading runs so contrary to long-standing traditions of interpretation of Luke–Acts, and yet the matter seems obvious in retrospect. Luke–Acts assumes and affirms the continuing election of faithful Israel, now reconstituted through the gift of repentance as bestowed by the Spirit, but it is the status of the gentile converts among the elect that remains at issue in Luke's community. Still sensitive to accusations from without by nonmessianist Jews and conscious of an extended and complex debate among believers, Luke–Acts presents the contested case that in accepting the Gentiles *as Gentiles,* the church is nevertheless faithful to "Moses and the prophets" since the Gentiles have now been "cleansed" by the Holy Spirit, who thus "made no distinction between us and them" (Acts 15:8–9).

That the inclusion of the Gentiles was the cause of grave accusations and persecution against the church by nonmessianists is still reflected in the polemics of the later chapters of Acts. The question of who is faithful and who is apostate is sharply drawn. Apart from remarks that the nonmessianists were simply inspired by jealousy at the success of messianist preaching (see 5:17; 13:45; 17:5), which is itself probably a countercharge of unfaithfulness (see Acts 7:9), the content of the accusations against Paul is not only the general abrogation of the law and offense against the temple (see Stephen, Acts 6:13–14). It is rather the inclusion of Gentiles or Greeks which constitutes the central offense. The "defense speeches" of Paul repeatedly emphasize that significant divisions exist among the Jews on many issues and that the "sects" of the Pharisees and the Nazarenes are even allies on the issue of the resurrection (23:6–10; 24:1–21). But the charge that Paul "brought Greeks into the temple" comprised his sin against "the people, the law and this place" (21:28), and even his mention of being charged with a mission to the Gentiles stirs up violent opposition, culminating in the refusal to "hear" him further (22:21–22; 24:6). Thus, in rehearsing the whole affair of his arrest one last time before Agrippa, Paul is depicted as stressing that it was indeed the message of repentance as extended to the Gentiles that caused his arrest. Yet he insists that in this "I stand here testifying both to small and great, saying nothing but what the prophets and Moses said would come to pass" (26:22). Apparently along with continuing hermeneutical debate concerning whether "the Messiah must suffer" (author's translation; see Luke 24:26,46; Acts 3:18; 17:3; 26:23) and argumentation that he was "the first to rise from the dead," the proclaiming of "light both to the people and to the Gentiles" provoked the sharpest controversy (26:23; see Luke 2:32).

The crucial ground on which these disputed questions were to be argued was, therefore, "Moses and the prophets," and Luke's presentation of the messianist hermeneutic of the fulfillment of all the scriptures in Jesus admits continuing disputation. "What is written in the law?" and "How do you read?" (Luke 10:26) are acknowledged as distinct questions. Simply "having Moses and the prophets" may not not be the same as "hearing Moses and the prophets" and repenting (Luke 16:29–31; see also 24:26–27,32; Acts 8:31; 13:27; 15:21). The issue of who has the "key of knowledge" (Luke 11:52) and who is misleading the people is thus joined by Luke in the many accounts of scriptural debates in the synagogues. "Examining the scriptures daily to see if these things were so" (Acts 17:11) stands in contrast with "jealousy" which prevents further hermeneutical debate (13:45; 17:5) as well as with attempts at entrapment (Luke 11:54; 14:1–3; 20:1–7,19; 21:27–40). At best, the views of this "sect which is everywhere spoken against" (Acts 28:22) would produce division in the house of Israel (see Luke 12:49–56). But even the indictment for disbelief would be couched in scriptural interpretive terms as a matter of "seeing and not seeing" and "hearing and not hearing." The hermeneutical battle lines are sharply drawn, and the case for the gentile mission must be made in the midst of such debate (see Acts 28:25–29).

Luke's account also discloses that the "gentile question" was the occasion for deep dispute among "believers" within the church as well as intra-Jewish attacks on "the Way." Indeed, the same "thousands among the Jews . . . who have believed" have been incorrectly advised (*katēchēthēsan*) that Paul is teaching "apostasy from Moses" for Jews who are among Gentiles (Acts 21:17–26, author's translation). Thus, James encourages Paul to display his faithful observance to these zealous Jewish Christians. Furthermore, in Acts 15 it is those "believers who belonged to the party of the Pharisees" who insisted that gentile converts were to be circumcised and charged to keep the law of Moses, precipitating the Jerusalem council. It may even be that this is where the reader is brought particularly close to the matter on which Luke is most concerned to provide the sure grounding for earlier instruction (*katēchēthēs,* Luke 1:4). The larger context could even suggest that what Luke feared from "the fierce wolves . . . speaking perverse things," mentioned in Paul's valedictory to the Ephesian elders (20:18–35), would have been the diminishing of the testimony of repentance to God and of faith in the Lord Jesus Christ which was to be declared *"both to Jews and to Greeks."*

Luke's persistent presentation of Paul and the apostles as observant Jews suggests a serious effort to eliminate any "misunderstanding" concerning the faithfulness of Jewish messianists to the law or their respect for the temple. The concern is so emphatic that the Paul in Acts who circumcises Timothy (16:3), takes a Nazarite vow (18:18), submits to ritual purification in accord with the scruples of James and the elders (21:17–27), and continues to present himself as a Pharisee (22:3; 23:6) is all but unrecognizable in the Paul of the letters. But the point is clear: faithfulness to the law is incumbent on all Jewish Christians.

Yet Luke also presents the admission of Gentiles as a distinctive mark of the Holy Spirit's work. As has been shown dramatically in Larrimore C. Crockett's studies of Jewish-gentile relations in Luke–Acts, it is "the fact of Jews and gentiles living and eating together" which constitutes the eschatological sign of the Spirit's activity.[52] Furthermore, Crockett has demonstrated that Luke's peculiar versions of the texts from Isaiah 61 and Kings not only accommodate his literary structure but also specify the application of these traditions to a current situation in the church.

Crockett's argument is detailed and carefully drawn, showing how, by means of Luke's combination of Isaiah 61 and Isaiah 58, the specific concern of the elect sharing their bread with the hungry is part of the program of the inclusion of the Gentiles.

> By the technique of enriching, Is. 58:6–7, which in its own context is an exhortation to social justice, becomes material to fill out the

meaning of the allusion to the messianic banquet in Is. 61:6. In this way, the phrase "good news to the poor" comes to have very concrete meaning and at the same time takes on the connotation of the messianic banquet.[53]

This concern is further developed in the repeated treatment of the strange assemblage of persons who are "invited" or "chosen" (*keklē-menoi*) to participate in table fellowship by Jesus (see Luke 7 and 14). Thus, Jesus' prophetic critique insists on the inclusion of the Gentiles in table fellowship against any narrow concept of the elect.[54]

Again, the Elijah story which Luke appropriates is shown by Crockett to reflect a pre-Lucan midrashic tradition in which a "gracious" Elijah was developed in part by the introduction of Isaiah texts, including Isa. 61:1, an Elijah "who in contrast to his stern and zealous nature as a prophet, returns to bring about reconciliation, forgiveness and resurrection."[55] In Luke's narrative, therefore, the famine under Elijah extending "over all the earth" represents a Lucan addition to broaden the scope of Elijah's symbolic mission to the Gentiles. It functions to anticipate a second "Spirit inspired event" when another famine "over the whole world" (Acts 11:28) would see the gentile Christians caring for and feeding the Jewish Christian community in Jerusalem, confirming that "to the Gentiles also God has granted repentance unto life" (11:18). The mission of the Jewish prophet serving the Gentiles both because of and in spite of the rejection of his own people eventually comes full circle with the Gentiles caring for and feeding Israel.

The affirmation that the Gentiles are to be included as Gentiles, even in the table fellowship, is thus a difficult issue within the community to which the scriptural resources must be addressed, and it is a crucial grounds for the charge of apostasy leveled against the messianists by other Jews. Just as the debate concerning the "true prophet" after the pattern of Deuteronomy 18 is implicit in Luke 4, so also the question of who in Israel is faithful to Moses and the prophets lies close at hand. But the evangelist is not only denouncing nonbelievers, he is also reciting these traditions in such a way that neither Jews nor Gentiles can exercise an exclusive claim to divine election.

Intolerance for those who are judged unfaithful, of course, will always leave the prophet and his oracles open to the charge of self-righteousness. Denouncing a misunderstanding of God's election unavoidably involves a claim to a more correct view or practice. But the integrity of the prophetic critique depends greatly on whether it is offered somehow "from within" so that it reflects the investment and vulnerability of the speaker rather than merely displaying the lofty superiority of an outsider. The force of the critique is also qualified and intensified by its ability to display self-criticism whether it be in rebukes against the pride of the new "elect" or the prophet's own sense of anguish, doubt, and perplexity concerning the human situation. And ultimately the prophetic diagnosis gains its compelling power from its vision of God who in full divine majesty, judgment, and grace has chosen a people and has chosen to relate and to continue to be involved with them. No simple theory of historical causation, fate, or rewards and punishments will be adequate to this theological vision. As Heschel states it, "Exceedingly intricate are his ways. Any attempt to formulate a theory, to stamp a dogma, to define God's itinerary through history, is a sham, fraught with pretension. In the realm of theology, shallowness is treason."[56]

The literary and hermeneutical complexity of Luke 4 which has been explored earlier is thus itself testimony to the subtlety and care with which the story is wrought. The matter is laid out: the clear disclosure of divine intention, the critical pause when faith or obduracy are being determined, the critical question, diagnosed immediately as implicit rejection, with the ensuing shower of prophetic oracles. At the same time, the scriptural backdrop furnished here and elsewhere by the evangelist makes the reader aware of larger theological issues, and these resist categorical solutions.

God's anointed ruler-prophet is heralding his eschatological reign. The validity of his word will receive its confirmation, but the soteriological question "Will the elect 'hear'?" is still unresolved. And when, in due time, many in Israel do respond in faith, how is the rejection of others to be understood, especially when the inclusion of the Gentiles continues to be such an offense to many Jews, both messianist and nonmessianist?

The passage is another microcosm of the whole of Luke–Acts, a "gospel in the Gospel." But it does not "explain" why Jesus was rejected, nor does it "explain" why the prophet turns against his audience except as these concerns are projected against a scriptural backdrop. The silences are poignant, drawing generations of interpreters into rash attempts to try to fill them. To be sure, the scriptural heritage has begun to diagnose what is going on, and the concern of the manifestation of God's purposes and the disclosure of human rejection is less cryptically presented than in Simeon's two-edged oracles that came before. In one sense, the grim conclusion of this episode alerts the reader that a dire fate awaits this prophet, and yet the stories of faith in Israel which follow immediately demonstrate that the rest of the tale is not a relentless slide toward tragedy.

Amid the unfaith and the faith of the people of God, the reign of God has come and is being deployed by his anointed prophet-king. His "destiny" or, more properly, his *mission* is inextricably bound up with the "destiny" or, better, the *calling* of the people.

"But the Samaritans Would Not Receive Him Because . . ."

Luke 9:51–56 must also be acknowledged as a programmatic restatement of the evangelist's understanding of the disclosure of divine intention and its consequent human rejection. Whether the larger outline of the gospel narrative is described in theological, literary, historical, or geographical terms, the critical placement of this episode rounding off Jesus' early ministry in Galilee and inaugurating his move toward Jerusalem is commonly recognized. Indeed, the complexity of the passage in its thematic and linguistic ties with the rejection in Nazareth, the descent from the mountain of transfiguration where the projected "exodus" was announced, and the anticipated entrance into Jerusalem already marks it as a carefully constructed turning point that will sustain thorough assessment. But a brief review of its literary and hermeneutical aspects must suffice for the purposes of this study.

Perhaps Luke 9:51 should be identified more specifically as the turning point, since it provides the narrative link binding the episode of Jesus' rejection by the Samaritans to the preceding story of the alien exorcist. However, if it is agreed that this transitional sentence is a Lucan composition, its vocabulary and syntax are so thoroughly integrated into the sentences following that the entire episode must be regarded in the light of that purposive sentence. Once again, the intention and commission of the prophet-king are clearly revealed and the rejection of another para-Jewish constituency, the Samaritans, is also manifested.[57]

But these disclosures are presented in such archaic phrases and freighted vocabulary that the reader is immediately alerted by the ponderously formal style to the momentous nature of the occasion. As in the opening sentence of the Gospel or the elaborate account of the ritualized preparations in the synagogue at Nazareth, once more the evangelist has built up a literary framework that marks the portent of what follows. Furthermore, the linguistic parallels between this passage and the work of the deuteronomistic historians as translated in the Septuagint compel the reader to perceive the episode against a scriptural background. Perhaps the effect is best captured by a consciously imitative "King James Bible" English translation of the text which seeks to preserve the puns on the terms of "going" and "face" as reflective of intentionality:

> And it came to pass that the days of his assumption were fulfilled. And he set his *face* to *go unto Jerusalem*. And he dispatched messengers before his *face*. And having *gone*, they entered into a village of Samaritans in order to prepare for his arrival. But they would not receive him because his *face* was *going unto Jerusalem*. And when his disciples James and John had seen this, they said, "Lord, is it your will that we should call fire to descend from heaven and consume them?" But he turned and rebuked them, and they did *go* unto another village. (Emphasis added, author's translation)

Again, since this passage is generally recognized as the formalized introduction to the "central section" or "travel narrative" of the gospel, its burdened prose can be best unpacked by reading on through the journey to its literary culmination with Jesus' arrival in Jerusalem. Certainly the ambiguous reference to his being "received up" (*analēmpsis*) in connection with his determination to go unto Jerusalem not only recalls the equally ambiguous reference to his "exodus" which he was "to fulfill in Jerusalem" (9:31), but also creates an "end stress" in the narrative. The reader is caught pondering when this mission will finally be accomplished. Is it when he is near Jerusalem and he says to Zacchaeus, "Today salvation has come to this house, since he is also a son of Abraham. For the Son of man came to seek and to save the lost" (19:9–10)?[58] Is it when the journey of the king has run its course and the judgment on those who would not receive him can be delayed no longer? (19:27–28, author's translation: " 'But as for these enemies of mine, who did not want me to reign over them, bring them here and slay them before me.' And when he had said this he did *go* on ahead, ascending [*anabainein*] unto Jerusalem.") Or is it after the multitude of disciples have hailed his approach to the city as that of "the King who comes in the name of the Lord" while the Pharisees, displaying their tragic blindness that the "time of visitation" has now indeed come, have suggested that Jesus again "rebuke" his disciples (19:39–44)? Or is this "way" only completed when it has led through the conflict, arrest, trial, execution, burial, and resurrection of Jesus in Jerusalem and he has been exalted in his assumption as Christ and Lord?[59] Or does it still await its consummation when the judgment will be visited on cities who have not received this "Lord" or his emissaries (9:54; 10:13–16)? No single view of the fulfillment appears adequate to Luke's presentation of the purposeful journey which is so explicitly renewed in this passage.[60] Furthermore, the paranetic function of such diverse travel stories as Homer's *Odyssey,* Israel's exodus, or a host of other excursions through natural and supernatural regions[61] strongly suggests that the symbolic value of Jesus' "going" on this "way" (see 9:57) be also assessed as thinly disguised counsel for the followers of "The Way."[62] This prolonged approach to Jerusalem therefore provides occasion for elaborate treatment of the themes of faithful discipleship between the pointed reminders of the goal that stands in the second and third passion predictions.[63] The section also strikes a distinctive balance between purposive or even urgent movement toward the end and the attending to a host of needs and homely matters of faithful practice along the way.

Such general literary observations are immediately helpful for interpreting the dynamics of this portion of the narrative, but they gain the force of greater particularity when their close correspondence to the book of Deuteronomy is recognized and correlated to the literary analysis. Even so, the fit is not exact. The narrative genre of the gospel would itself preclude any simple imitation of Moses' parting catechesis of Israel. Some of the correlations with Deuteronomy are still so general that they could be fortuitous or automatic to any account of the departing leader's preparation of the people. Moreover, the hellenistic model of the wandering philosopher and his disciples would certainly have come to mind for many first-century readers. Thus, reference to this section of Luke as a "Christian Deuteronomy" may often only be a comment about its ethical counsel in comparison with other farewell discourses, testaments, or instructions to disciples "on the way."

But the case is considerably stronger. As C. F. Evans argues in his essay on "The Central Section of St. Luke's Gospel," Luke's presentation of Jesus as a "prophet like Moses" permeates his account of this deliberate approach to Jerusalem. Furthermore, Evans fortifies his analysis by pointing to several striking resemblances between Luke–Acts and the "Testament of Moses." He suggests that the evangelist might have been familiar with the Testament book in its final form as the Assumption of Moses.

> He will have been acquainted with a document which under the title of *analēmpsis* comprised not only the passage of its subject from earth to heaven by a mysterious death, but also a series of addresses and injunctions delivered in Amman beyond Jordan to his successor whom he is leaving behind.[64]

The possibility of such direct literary dependence providing the basis for interpreting Jesus' preparation for the fulfillment of his *analēmpsis* in Luke is indeed enticing. And closer study of the figure of Moses in the Testament both reveals further analogies with Luke's presentation of Jesus in this section and suggests crucial contrasts.[65] Certainly Moses the faithful prophet who intercedes and suffers on behalf of his people and whose prophecy attests to the primordial divine plan in Israel's history represents a midrashic adaptation of Deuteronomony that illumines Luke's appropriation of the same scriptural traditions. When the Testament is viewed as a rewriting of Moses' predictive history of Israel (Deuteronomy 31–34) in comparison with other contemporary rewritings of the same material (i.e.,

Jubilees 1, pseudo-Philo's *Biblical Antiquities* 19, Josephus's *Antiquities* IV 302–31), it becomes clear that the recapitulation of Moses' parting words to his successor Joshua/Jesus was a lively medium for continuing discussion concerning God's involvement in Israel's history. As Daniel Harrington has shown, the deuteronomic pattern of apostasy, punishment, and vindication is commonly assumed to these rehearsals and brought to bear in discrete diagnoses of what sin constitutes Israel's apostasy and of how God will deal with it.[66]

The similarities between Luke–Acts and the Testament therefore point beyond possible literary dependence and even beyond common reference to Deuteronomy. What comes into view is an *ongoing hermeneutical debate* concerning Israel's faithfulness to Moses' instruction, upon which Israel's continuing election depends. This debate reflects sharply conflicting opinions concerning the specific diagnosis of Israel's "apostasy" or "idolatry." Although this intra-Jewish discussion had currency throughout the era of the second temple, its poignancy no doubt increased with the destruction of Jerusalem. Imagine, for example, the distress the faithful would have felt after the destruction when they read the melancholy confessions as 1 Baruch, with their direct citation of the "curse which the Lord declared through his servant Moses" (1:20; see Deuteronomy 28; Jer. 11:3–5).

It will not be possible within this study to pursue the spectrum of views concerning what constitutes faithfulness and apostasy, although that investigation promises to reveal diverse self-understandings within Israel in considerable detail. But it is at least necessary to note that the "gentile question" is always close at hand, perhaps especially in Deuteronomy, where the "abomination of the Gentiles" becomes a basic definition of the idolatry and apostasy of the false prophet against which the "prophet like Moses" stands (see especially 18: 9–22; 13:1–18). In Deuteronomy, furthermore, the nations are viewed almost exclusively in the light of their being instrumental to God's judgment or blessing of Israel. Second Isaiah's vision of the preserved of Israel serving as a light to the Gentiles so that divine salvation may reach to the "end of the earth" (*heōs eschatou tēs gēs:* 49:6, 45:22) probably inspired Luke's vision of the mission of the church (Acts 1:8). Zechariah's oracle concerning the Gentiles as being one nation in Jerusalem (Zech. 14:16–19) may also be reflected at several points in his narrative. Yet such views stand in sharp contrast with the text of Deuteronomy in which the "ends of the earth" are where God pushes the Gentiles "all of them."[67] Thus, while the promise-fulfillment theology of true prophecy in the deuteronomistic traditions has been thoroughly appropriated, a broader selection of prophetic texts has been invoked to include the Gentiles in the divine economy of salvation.

The book of Jubilees, by contrast, uses the deuteronomic pattern with a singular emphasis on repentance. It is specifically the "walking after the Gentiles and after their uncleanness" (1:9) from which the hearts of the children of Israel must be cleansed by the creating of a holy spirit in them (1:21,23). Small wonder, therefore, that when Acts maintains that "repentance" is given to both Jews and Gentiles, the matter was subject to dispute. And when the story of Peter's vision of the common and unclean animals is repeatedly cited to demonstrate that "what God has cleansed, you must not call common"[68] (10:15; 11:9), it is clear that the author is leading up to a stand on the gentile question which would be categorically opposed to that in Jubilees on its same terms: "And God who knows the heart bore witness to them, giving them the Holy Spirit just as he did to us; and he made no distinction between us and them, but cleansed their hearts by faith" (Acts 15:8–9). To be sure, Luke 9:51–56 does not deal directly with the gentile question. That matter is taken up in Acts, where a defense must be made. But here Luke is presenting a sharply different diagnosis of faithlessness based on his reading of the same scriptural traditions. Both Jews and Samaritans are guilty of the apostasy of not receiving the prophet like Moses.

Thus, the affinities between Luke 9:51–56 and the opening chapters of Deuteronomy also appear in a new light. Although the scene can be credibly regarded as offering a subtle critique of those hellenistic kings, emperors, or "benefactors" who would "liberate" villages in their path by intimidation, its primary impact is in its careful appropriation of an authoritative scriptural tradition to promote a contested view. It is Moses the prophet, teacher, and ruler of Israel who provides the paradigm for Luke's presentation of Jesus: that is, the long-suffering Moses who prepares his people to "go" on the "way" before "the face" of the Lord after his departure,[69] who sends the twelve men on ahead, one from each tribe (Deut. 1:23), and who appoints seventy elders to share his spirit "and they shall bear the burden of the people with you, that you may not bear it yourself alone" (Num. 11:17; see Deut. 1:9; Luke 9:1–6,51–57; 10:1). Taken once again together with the figure of Elijah the prophet, whose power before the faithless of Israel was legendary (2 Kings 1), Luke's Jesus is disclosed in awesome proportions of authority.

Yet Luke's peculiar appropriation of these powerful images with their freighted vocabulary is best recognized by the way the volition of the agents is displayed. It is not simply a case of sending messengers "before his face" but also of his "setting his face." As in the firm resolve of the third "servant song" of Isa. 50:7, "I have set my face like a flint" (*sterean petran*), so now Jesus' face is set (*stērizein*) to go to Jerusalem. This metaphor for the prophetic vocation is also similar to Ezekiel's mission to Jerusalem: "Therefore prophesy son of men and set your face [*stērizein*] toward Jerusalem" (Ezek. 21:2; see also 21:1,LXX, author's translation).[70] Furthermore, Luke's second restatement of this resolve and vocation provides the only glimpse into why Jesus was not received by the Samaritans: "because his face was going unto Jerusalem."

Perhaps this rationale was also intended to allude to a specifically Samaritan objection to the Jerusalem goal of Jesus' mission or to anticipate the difficulty of following a prophet whose fate was already so dire. But the evangelist's poignant silence again cautions against too specific an explanation of a matter in which the ambiguity may be central to its calculated effect. The text does not elaborate the Samaritans' motivation so much as it depicts the offense of Jesus' carefully defined role. Whether it can be established that this introduction to a "Christian Deuteronomy" has been intentionally "enriched" by an allusion to the servant songs or Ezekiel, it is clear that as Luke presents this encounter, Jesus is rejected on precisely the terms in which his firm resolve has been expressed.

The rejection of Jesus is thus programmatic, a second archetypal encounter in which the prophet's mission in obedience to the divine will stands at odds with the people's willingness to concur. Faithfulness to the authoritative tradition is defined by the reception of this prophet and his mission, and the specifically Samaritan grounds of the refusal are only of secondary interest. Since the first two passion predictions stand in close connection with the announcement of the "exodus" and "assumption" which Jesus is about to "fulfill," the reader has been alerted to the way this "prophet like Moses" has determined to go.

This passage concerning the Samaritans must be considered along with Luke's treatment of the Samaritans in other contexts and in comparison with his presentation of Jews and Gentiles. The peculiar place that the Samaritans hold relative to Israel in Luke's account may already be reflected with the greatest clarity in the strategic placement of the Samaritan episodes within the narrative. These incidents do not only correspond to significant geographical developments (see especially Acts 1:6; 8:1–25). Just as Jesus' first public manifestation to his own people in Nazareth evokes rejection, so also is this rejection provoked when he first comes among the Samaritans. Both accounts are followed by specific examples of "faith" among Jews and Samaritans (e.g., the lepers in Luke 5:12–16; 17: 11–19), and the descent of the Spirit upon Israel at Pentecost is followed by the receiving of Christian preaching by the Samaritans as confirmed by the Spirit's descent (Acts 2 and 8). The Samaritans are no better nor worse than the Jews. Neither in Nazareth nor in the Samaritan villages is immediate judgment invoked, but their future is desperate unless there is repentance (see Luke 10:12–16; 13:1–5). Without the gift of repentance, neither the Jews nor the Samaritans could be part of restored Israel from which the mission to the Gentiles proceeds. The prophetic critique transcends ethnic lines.

Luke 9:51–56, therefore, provides another paradigm of the disclosure of the prophet's mission and its rejection by a people closely related to Israel. And why is the prophet rejected? Because the people are unwilling to accept his mission. But why? Because of Jerusalem? Because of the temple? Because of Jesus' unhappy prospects in that city? Tempting as it is to try to explicate the matter in greater detail, the evangelist stops short of tidy moral or psychological explanations of the specific motives or causes of the offense that has been taken. In fact, such pursuits may risk missing the larger theological issue that appears to be clear within the hermeneutical discussion of what constitutes Israel's faithfulness or unfaithfulness to the Mosaic charter. Especially in this section where the deuteronomistic pattern appears to have been adopted so thoroughly, the direct confrontation between the prophet's commission and the people's refusal is itself definitive. Exactly "why" the rejection has taken place may admit several interpretations, but the refusal of the prophet like Moses constitutes and reveals the grievous apostasy of both the Jews and the Samaritans.

3

Weeping for Jerusalem

The Fate of Jerusalem: A Long
Contested Question

Israel's scriptural tradition was itself forged in the heat of peril, shaped by the calamities of the Assyrian conquest of ancient Israel and the Babylonian destruction of Jerusalem and Judea, and wrought in the retrospect of diverse interpretations of those unhappy events. Any possibility that the scriptural interpretations of Israel's place in history, cherished and cultivated during the exile and catalyzed by the complexity of the "return" and restoration of Jerusalem, would become stereotyped or automatic was precluded by persistent new threats. Again and again, the sanctity of the temple and the integrity of the high priesthood were subject to desecration and defamation.

In the centuries of the hegemony of the hellenistic empires, a class of powerful, landed Jewish families made elaborate efforts to accommodate their traditions to the dominant culture, but the result was an internecine battle for control of the high priestly office, precipitating the attack of Antiochus IV Epiphanes who defiled the temple precincts with abominations and inaugurated a pogrom against observing Jews (c. 167 B.C.).[1] Although rallied for a brief time by this common enemy under the leadership of the Hasmonean Judas "Maccabeus" and his brothers, the diverse economic, religious, and political constituencies were again rapidly fragmented by the military and political policies of the new regime. Even before the temple was rededicated, disagreements emerged concerning the faithful conduct of holy warfare against the Gentiles and proper cultic observance. But when "the Jews and their priests decided that [Judas's brother] Simon should be their leader and high priest for ever, until a trustworthy prophet should appear" (1 Macc. 14:41), sectarian polemics against the "wicked priest" soon ensued along with an uneasy alliance between the priest-kings and the Pharisaic party.[2] When dissensions between two Hasmonean claimants to this royal-priestly office degenerated into civil war, the temple was once again besieged and defiled. This time the agent was the Roman general Pompey (63 B.C.), who was admitted to the city by one faction and resisted from within the temple by another until the wall was breached and the priests slaughtered. The manipulation of the high priesthood by Herod the Great and the unsuccessful attempts by Pilate and Caligula to introduce votive shields or the emperor's own effigy continued to provoke intense reactions and to prompt diverse speculations concerning the fate of the city and temple as related to Israel's faithfulness.

Up until and beyond the destruction by the Romans, Israel's scriptural heritage requiring its responsibility for its fortunes not only provided a unified field for such discussion but also increased its vulnerability to internal recriminations and mutual faultfinding. Under the duress of Rome's overwhelming power and Israel's own rapidly deteriorating political prospects, Israel's checkered history of valiant and vain efforts to purge its own uncleanness and to unburden itself of a series of yokes of oppression bequeathed to it a legacy with which to interpret the eminently predictable if not inevitable war with Rome. The degree to which the Roman destruction was interpreted in terms of the traditions of the ancient Babylonian destruction may be estimated by Josephus's report that while God had long since sentenced the temple and the fated city, the final conflagration was reserved for the precise anniversary of the first burning (*Wars* 6:250–67). The question of how those traditions were to be brought to bear was, nevertheless, fraught with division. And when Jerusalem eventually lay in ruins, the common ground for such disputes was all but irretrievable.

Luke's presentation of Jesus' oracles concerning Jerusalem must be regarded as part of this intense hermeneutical debate. At the same time, the probable impact of Jesus' own contribution to the question of the fate of Jerusalem ought not to be denied. No doubt any Jewish "prophet" of the era would have offered words of judgment or hope concerning the obvious peril of Jerusalem and Herod's temple within it. It is also remarkable how many of the diverse figures whom Josephus in retrospect calls "false prophets" or "impostors" can still be recognized as attempting to stir up a new "exodus" or otherwise liberate Israel from bondage, and some of these "prophets like Moses" even bore the name Joshua, that is, Jesus. Perhaps the most poignant of those presented by Josephus was the "rude peasant" named Joshua/Jesus who appeared at the feast of tabernacles four years before the war. His melancholy cry was reportedly a restatement of Jeremiah's refrain "a voice from the east, a voice from the west, a voice from the four winds, a voice against the bridegroom and the bride, a voice against all the people."[3] Josephus further reports that he recited this oracle unremittingly until during the siege, when he added "and woe to me also" and was struck dead by a Roman projectile.

To be sure, Josephus's account was composed after the fact of the destruction, and he marshals such stories to his purposes. But a *post eventum* literary composition does not mean that all such oracles had an *ex eventu* origin. Indeed, even the most skeptical reading of this history would acknowledge that Jewish scriptural traditions concerning God's protection and/or judgment of the city and the temple guaranteed that they would be the subject and focus of competitive interpretations of the times. Whether it was the covenanters withdrawing from the city and temple to Qumran to await divine intervention, the Pharisees actively scrutinizing temple sacrifices to ensure faithful observance, or the high priestly contingent in close alliance with the Sadducees defending the sanctity of current practices, ominous oracles and confident assurances of God's election were both endemic to the discussion. Certainly the broad gospel traditions attributing such remarks to Jesus and emphasizing the offense that they cause are quite credible historically.

The more pressing question for the present, however, is how did the evangelist appropriate such traditions, whatever their origin, for the purposes of his narrative? If a date after the destruction of Jerusalem seems most probable for Luke's composition, have the oracles concerning Jerusalem now been used so extensively at the expense of "the Jews" that a context outside the pale of Israel must be assumed?

The question does not admit easy answers but raises additional considerations. It must be granted, for example, that Luke's implied and expressed interpretation of the national crisis would have been thoroughly unacceptable to Jews who did not regard Jesus as the messiah, and his views of Jerusalem's fate were directly useful for gentile self-justification and triumphalist anti-Semitism. Once the church had become a gentile movement and the split with the synagogues was complete, the tears shed for Jerusalem were quickly exploited in attacks on "the Jews."[4] But, of course, Josephus's account as well as the oracles of Jeremiah and Micah were also ready grist for such mills, and 1 and 2 Baruch may be still more accusatory toward Israel in explicitly scriptural terms. Thus, the invocation of the sharply critical scriptural traditions of Deuteronomy and Jeremiah does not in itself set the evangelist over against Israel, particularly since the intra-Jewish debate concerning the election of this people is still vital.

It is also crucial to note that these oracles have not been so manipulated that a detailed fulfillment of Jesus' predictions has been documented by the events of the war with Rome. While agreeing that the narrative was probably composed after the destruction, C. H. Dodd has shown that Jesus' laments in Luke were wrought from the metal of traditional scriptural allusions rather than fashioned ex post facto to verify the prophecies by their correspondence to what actually happened: "So far as any historical event has coloured the picture, it is not Titus' capture of Jerusalem in A.D. 70 but Nebuchadnezzar's capture in 586 B.C. There is no single trait which cannot be documented directly out of the Old Testament."[5]

The possibility of the existence of a "Proto-Luke" or earlier draft of the gospel must also be considered in this regard in deference to the careful analysis of these Lucan passages offered by Lloyd Gaston. His investigations are of particular interest to this study since the same intra-Jewish interpretation assigned here to the whole of Luke–Acts is regarded by Gaston as characteristic of the pre-Lucan, prewar literary source that he seeks to reconstruct. Two brief quotes from Gaston must suffice:

> . . . the fall of Jerusalem in Proto-Luke is spoken of not as a future historical event but as a warning, a threat which the church still hopes will not happen. But even if the worst does happen, still the promises of God to Israel will not fail of fulfillment.
>
> What in Proto-Luke still was an alternative, . . . becomes in Luke a temporal succession: first salvation to part of Israel, then the fulfillment of the threat, then the fulfillment of the salvation for the Gentiles, and finally the end.[6]

Gaston's observation of the sequential staging of the past and future events has proved helpful, and his adoption of the Proto-Luke hypothesis has allowed the recognition of the sensitivity to the Jewish–Christian situation implicit in the text, although the prevailing interpretation of Luke's "salvation history" makes such concerns appear uncharacteristic of the evangelist. Yet the analysis falters exactly at the point of using the completed narrative as a foil to describe Proto-Luke. Both the massive extent of Gaston's Proto-Luke lectionary[7] and its thematic coherence serve to challenge those prevailing views of Luke's enterprise which are largely based on contrasts with Mark and on the polemics against "the Jews" in the speeches in Acts. But these same factors finally undermine the Proto-Luke hypothesis as well.

Instead of positing a contrasting source which is comprehensive in its contents, including much that is thoroughly Lucan, it is incumbent upon the interpreter to recognize that this larger framework is definitive of the composition as a whole. The "alterations" of Mark must be evaluated within the scope of the literary whole, not used first to describe Luke's purposes in Markan terms and secondly to define a new literary entity that has no independent attestation but comprises an extensive and critical portion of the completed work.

The effect of these observations, therefore, is once more to challenge certain long-standing assumptions concerning the occasion, purposes, and methods of Luke–Acts. That there is no explicitly post-destruction account does not prevent the likelihood that Jesus' oracles have been rehearsed to interpret the actual destruction, but it does caution against the view that the evangelist has coolly turned the traditions against Israel. The matter is more complex, and the concern for the continuity of God's election of Israel is expressed in the midst of experienced discontinuities. Again, if the intra-Jewish pathos and polemic can be regarded as intrinsic to the evangelist's purposes and not merely consigned to an earlier document, even the most caustic charges and recriminations may be accepted as within the bounds of prophetic pronouncements of weal and woe.

This study seeks to show that Luke's recitation of Jesus' oracles concerning Jerusalem constitutes the evangelist's interpretation of its destruction. Largely on the basis of probable dependence on Mark and the development of the theme of Jerusalem's dire fate, it appears most likely that the event is already past. But even the fact that the evangelist does not tip his hand overtly concerning details except by scriptural allusions is itself an indirect clue to his methods. He does offer an interpretation of the times which can be shown to be coherent, and it does arise from his theocentric convictions. Yet "theologian of history" may be a misnomer if that term implies a thoroughly consistent statement *about* history. Rather, Luke works in the medium of story and tradition, building a composite framework within which the lived experience of the community may be interpreted.[8] And that community is still very much caught up in the pain and plight of post-destruction Jewish groups contending with their tragic history in the light of their scriptural heritage.

"I Must Go . . . For a Prophet Must Not Die Outside Jerusalem"

Luke 13:31–35 is literarily complex in spite of its brevity. As in 9:51–56, it appears that the evangelist has provided a transitional sentence of introduction which not only ties the pericope into its context but also introduces the subject matter which is then explored with a series of repeated words or puns. Simply reading the text on such a level already makes it another episode in which a conflict of wills is disclosed. The question of who will direct Jesus' "going" (*poreuesthai*) and whose intentions (*thelein*) shall be accomplished thus serves to introduce a lament which is also replete with scriptural phrases and allusions.

> At that same hour, certain Pharisees approached and said to him, "Depart and *go* from here, for Herod *intends* to kill you." And he said to them, "No, you *go* and say to that fox, 'Behold I am casting out demons and I am *accomplishing* [*apotelein*] cures today, tomorrow, and on the third day I will (be) *complete* [*teleioumai*]. Moreover *it is necessary* that I *go* on my way today, tomorrow, and the day following for *it is not acceptable* that a prophet perish outside of *Jerusalem*.
>
> "*Jerusalem, Jerusalem,* who kills the prophets and stones those dispatched to her. How often I have *intended* to gather your children as a bird takes her own brood under her wings, yet you did not so *intend*. Behold your house is forsaken to you. But I say to you, you shall not see me until [it will come when] you say to me, 'Blessed is the one who comes in the name of the Lord.'" (Emphasis added, author's translation)

Here the evangelist provides another highly detailed picture of an exchange with an economy of words. He highlights Jesus' sharp rejection of the Pharisees' suggestion as completely inappropriate. When Jesus' words to the Pharisees are coupled with the lament, they identify such warnings as part and parcel of the ominous rejection of the prophet which bodes so ill for Jerusalem. The severity of Jesus' response is also noteworthy, particularly since the phrase "How often I would have gathered" Jerusalem has no literary warrant in this context. At least in Matthew's gospel, Jesus has been in the temple and city for some time before the lament is uttered (Matt. 23:37–39).

But in Luke, Jesus' rejoinder is so abrupt and ominous that the shaken reader may join company with many of the commentators to try to "explain" what was really going on. Were the Pharisees sincere in their warning, or had they trumped up a threat to try to deter Jesus from his mission? Was Herod actually intent on killing Jesus (see 3:19; Acts 4:27) or merely perplexed and curious (see 9:9; 23:7–12)? But Luke stops short of expounding their motives. Indeed, a host of preceding stories render mute any attempt to assess the moral or psychological "causes." The uncompromising prophetic indictment resists trivial theodicies concerning why the Galileans were killed by Pilate or the eighteen victims in Siloam died while others were spared. Instead it unleashes wrath on the pious disapproval of sabbath healing (13:1–5,10–17). Jesus' cutting response to these "certain Pharisees" stands as Luke's illustration of the kind of judgment that has been pronounced "at that very hour" (v. 31). Their apparently "helpful advice" is immediately turned against them, just as those who presumed themselves to be elect suddenly found themselves excluded from the household and banquet of the eschatological reign of God. The suggestion of these Pharisees is interpreted as an effort to divert Jesus from accomplishing his purpose, thereby disclosing the culpable rejection of the prophet.

The allusive and ambiguous language of 31–35 also contributes to the import of the passage as something of a midpoint in the journey, renewing the movement toward fulfilling Jesus' "exodus" or "assumption" in Jerusalem and thus anticipating his "completion." It has even been argued that "the Lucan journey falls into a chiastic pattern" with 31–33 and 34–35 standing at the intersection.[9] At any rate, when Luke's Jesus speaks of "fulfilling" or "being completed" on the third day, this unusual passive is first explicated by the following sentence in which "going" on the third day is repeated in reference to the prophet perishing in Jerusalem. Then Luke's distinctive use of the cognate term *telein* in the third passion prediction must be regarded as further commentary: "Behold we are going up [ascending] unto Jerusalem and all the things written through the prophets concerning the son of man *shall be accomplished*" (Luke 18:31, emphasis added; author's translation). Along with the "exodus" and "assumption," Jesus' "baptism" which constrains him until it is "accomplished" (*telein,* 12:50) is later interpreted for the reader in terms of the prophetic-scriptural agenda of the accomplishment of the divine will. But even then, Luke states from three vantage points that "they did not understand . . . and this word was hidden from them . . . and they did not know" (18:34, author's translation). Not even the twelve are privy to the divine purposes which are disclosed only by oblique allusions that the reader may spot in retrospect of their accomplishment. The problem of "knowing" is not a simple matter of willful choice, but it is also caught up in the theological concern of testifying to a God who pursues declared purposes within history in spite of, because of, and through human agency.

Beyond the apparent "misplacement" of the lament and the obscure reference to the "completion" in Jerusalem, however, the evangelist has also provided another advance signal in his recitation of the oracle. Its final phrase, "Blessed is he who comes in the name of the Lord" now stands in this context as an ominous parting remark, set against this effort to deter him from his course and serving notice that not only does Jerusalem's fate already look dim, but if the city is ever to "see" this prophet it will be at the time when[10] this crucial phrase is uttered. Thus, in Jesus' "ascent into Jerusalem" (19:28) when Luke presents "the whole multitude of the disciples praising God with a loud voice for all the mighty works they had *seen*," their rephrasing of this allusion to Psalm 118 becomes all the more portentous: "Blessed is he who comes in the name of the Lord, *the King!*" (19:38, emphasis added). The next suggestion of "some of the Pharisees" to Jesus that he rebuke his disciples for such acclamation (19:39) will then evoke a second and still more decisive lament over Jerusalem with no possibility of a "seeing" (19:41–44; see the next section of this chapter). Simply on a literary level, therefore, it is clear that Luke 13:31–35 has been structured in close correlation to the third Gospel's account of Jesus' entry into Jerusalem where the suspense of this earlier pericope is largely resolved.

Yet this is not simply a literary artifice, nor is the opposition to Jesus displayed by "some of the Pharisees" (see also 6:2) merely accounted for or dismissed as due to spite or some other base motive. Indeed if the polemics of non-Lucan traditions against the Pharisees are not allowed to cloud the discussion, the theological and hermeneutical debates with the Pharisees and accusations of hypocrisy in the practice of the law still may be intense. But no usual caricature of the Pharisees as opponents will do justice to the complexity and seriousness of the disputes that Jesus and later the apostles have with them, including those Pharisees who are "believers" and those who stand with the messianists in the debates concerning the resurrection (see Luke 20:27–39; Acts 15:5; 23:7–9; 5:34–39). Within Luke's narrative, it is in fact quite possible to ascribe good intentions to these "certain Pharisees" who warn Jesus about Herod and to recognize that their counsel concerning the extravagance and danger of the disciples' behavior could be construed as simply prudent. The reader may see their error, but how were they to know? Were they "worse sinners" than the ignorant disciples (see 18:34)?

Once again the scriptural bases of the story must be located in order to attempt a more adequate description of what is happening in Luke's narrative. For crucial as the opposition of "some of the Pharisees" is to the specific course of events that follows, the decisive action flows from two verbs that are impersonal in form and qualify Jesus' "completion" on the third day as contrasted with the intentions of Herod according to the counsel of the Pharisees. "Nevertheless *it is necessary* that I go today and tomorrow and on the day after for *it is not fitting* for a prophet to perish outside Jerusalem" (emphasis added, author's translation).

As was noted previously in the discussion of Simeon's oracles concerning the child who was "set for the fall and rising of many in Israel," Luke's predilection for such passive and impersonal language concerning "agency" must be acknowledged as consistent with a general Jewish aversion to speaking directly of God. However, a complicated contemporary discussion concerning the predetermination and causation of historical events also comes quickly into view. Indeed, even when the scriptural warrant for Lucan statements of *necessity* is explicitly identified as fundamental to the purposes and structuring of the narrative,[11] the crucial questions of "canonics,"[12] or which authoritative traditions are used and how they are used, must be raised.

The appeal to ostensibly ancient texts and oracles on the grounds that "it is written" was common to many cultural traditions in the hellenistic world. Furthermore, the spectrum of views concerning how such traditions were to be invoked was broad. The cosmology and eschatology of a given interpretation was often more definitive of its place in the spectrum than the ethnic origin or peculiar lectionary of its author. The task is not to decide which approaches are "hellenistic" and which are "biblical"[13] since "most holy Plato" and Moses may be cited in chorus or the oracles of the Sibyl may be infused with

Jewish monotheism. But the ways authoritative traditions are used to qualify and interpret the contested ground of history can be described with discrimination.

All the affinities which Luke–Acts shares with Greco-Roman historiography for speaking of *necessity, causation,* and *testimony* must be carefully noted along with the novelistic interest in characterization and dramatization that is shared with ancient nationalistic romance literature. Still, its peculiarly Jewish hermeneutical lectionary and agenda are fundamental to any description of Luke–Acts. Like 1 Maccabees or Josephus, Luke draws heavily upon the deuteronomistic historical traditions to interpret recent history. His lectionary is not that of the apocalyptic traditions of Daniel and Qumran and his hermeneutic is not that of the Platonism of Philo of Alexandria. Although aware of certain conventions in contemporary historiography, he is less attracted than Josephus to the rhetoric and vocabulary of the Greek and Roman histories. And when he does express the complexities of agency in impersonal verbs and passive constructions, it is not to counsel resignation to arbitrary fates and forces. Rather, it is to confront the reader with the determined purpose of "God, the faithful God who keeps covenant and steadfast love with those who love him and keep his commandments, to a thousand generations, and requites to their face those who hate him, by destroying them" (Deut. 7:9–10).

In the case of the "central section" of Luke, the connections with the book of Deuteronomy itself may even have been carefully calculated. As mentioned above, C. F. Evans has attempted to trace a correlation of subject matter. James A. Sanders has also argued that the section presents Luke's version of Jesus' "prophetic critique of current inversions of the Deuteronomic ethic of election."[14] Others have referred generally to its quality as a "Christian Deuteronomy" because of the agglomeration of ethical catecheses under the literary guise of the impending "departure" of the prophet. The possibility of an unobtrusive "running commentary" on Deuteronomy in this section certainly invites a more thorough exploration of the ways in which the scriptures were used in the synagogues of the hellenistic world as crucial media for arguing and for arbitrating conflicting claims and views among various parties. Such observations at least suggest that this elaborate and enriched story of Jesus' approach to Jerusalem must not be reduced to a simple series of "proof texts" in an attack on the Jews.[15]

Thus, whether or not it can be shown that the evangelist was constructing a commentary on Deuteronomy out of Christian traditions concerning Jesus, or a commentary on Jesus' ministry following the outline of Deuteronomy, it is clear that the contents of those scriptural allusions are *not incidental* to his literary purposes. The strategic impersonal verbs, standing in sharp contrast to the suggestions of "certain Pharisees," indicate that obedience to the prophet's vocation and God's intention as disclosed in the scripture immediately set Jesus at odds with their views. Whether or not they could or were expected to perceive what was at stake, by means of the allusions the reader is privy to Luke's retrospective presentation of Jesus' premonitory interpretation of the encounter.

The gloomy traditions concerning the suffering of God's prophets and messengers which long characterized deuteronomistic traditions had apparently been transmitted to Luke through the rhetoric of the suffering of God's Wisdom and its offspring (see Luke 11:37–54). Although the scriptural warrant for the charge that Israel and specifically Jerusalem killed the prophets is extremely thin, in certain intertestamental literature it had apparently become an accepted diagnosis of the evils that had been visited upon Israel.[16] Thus, such a *topos* is not merely a gentile invective. As it has been set into Luke's literary framework, probably out of Q, it represents the evangelist's use of an available "scriptural" tradition to emphasize once again that the rejection of the prophet constitutes the culpable error of Israel and Jerusalem, the people of God.

The traditional lament is itself already filled with scriptural allusions; and since the correspondence with Matthew's version of the oracle is remarkably close, it is clearly impossible to know how self-consciously all of the scriptural elements were thought to serve Luke's distinctive purposes. The melange of references to the gathering and the wasting of the "house" and the chorus of the last of the great Egyptian Hallel psalms to welcome the king to the temple constituted a complex hermeneutical assessment of Jerusalem's plight (see also Jer. 22:5; 12:7). Yet long before, the Song of Moses (Deuteronomy 32) had already depicted the pathos of the prophet as caught up in the anguish of God who fluttered over Israel like a bird leading Israel out of Egypt only then to be provoked by its unfaithfulness. This rich collection of images of divine protection and jealous wrath over unfaithfulness was certainly not original with the evangelist or Jesus.

By its placement, however, Luke has explicated the strange little episode of the conflict of wills with "certain Pharisees" and escalated it into a foreshadowing of Jesus' conflict in Jerusalem. Indeed, verses 31 to 33 are probably best understood as Luke's own composition to provide an occasion to lend particularity to the traditional oracles. In Matthew's context, the concluding refrain from Psalm 118 would appear to anticipate an eschatological appearance, since it is a threat followed by his departure from the temple. In Luke, however, the refrain explicates the conflict with these Pharisees in anticipation of a critical encounter within the story that looms ahead. Now the phrase "you will not see me until you say" anticipates that some will indeed say, "Blessed is he who comes" and will "see him." Thus, Luke has created a mood of anticipation and a subtle scriptural interpretation of that impending conflict.

In this context, the lament and the sharp reproof of those "certain Pharisees" mutually reinforce the same view present in Simeon's oracles, in Jesus' sermon in Nazareth, and in the encounter with the Samaritan villages. Jesus' course and vocation allow no dissimulation and accommodate no diversion. The conflict of wills, the disclosure of the "secret thoughts of the hearts" is apparently unavoidable and purposive. As with the divine visitation in and through the prophets of old in Israel, the awesome divine will to preserve may, for a time, destroy. Its saving and redeeming purpose may indeed be obscured in wrath and destruction. The peril is immense for "a perverse generation, children in whom is no faithfulness. . . . I would have said, 'I will scatter them afar, I will make the remembrance of them cease from among men' " (Deut. 32:20,26; see also Luke 9:41; Acts 2:40). So in Luke, the stakes are incredibly high! The structure of the narrative reinforces this fact by stressing that it is the rejection of Jesus the prophet like Moses that indicts Israel. The question remains, however, has Israel become merely an object of divine wrath or is even the judgment on Jerusalem prefatory to cleansing and restoration?

"For You Did Not Know: Now They Are Hid from Your Eyes"

Jesus' tears for Jerusalem in Luke 19:41–44 might well have evoked associations with similar scenes of pathos in the moralistic and tragic histories so much in vogue in the hellenistic world. Luke's foreshadowing of this passage might even have won him praise for its literary artistry. But if the warp of the story would have thus been discernible according to such broader cultural standards, its weft could only have been properly assayed by those who knew the scriptures of the hellenistic synagogues. It is finally the sympathy of the suffering prophet, of Deuteronomy's Moses, of Jeremiah, Isaiah, and Hosea, caught up in the rage, anguish, frustration, and sorrow of God for Israel that constitutes the pathos of this story.

The pericope stands at a critical juncture in the whole narrative and delineates the themes sounded previously in 13:31–35. If the acclamation of Jesus by his disciples as "the king who comes in the name of the Lord" on his approach to Jerusalem marks the "fulfillment" of his purposive journey, then the response by those "certain Pharisees" (19:39–40) and Jesus' ensuing remarks (vv. 41–44) provide a weighty interlude between the end of the "travel narrative" and Jesus' dramatic entry into the temple. Without speculating concerning what Jesus himself might have had in mind or attempting to reconstruct possible earlier stages of Christian tradition behind these verses, it is clear that their pivotal-transitional function serves Luke's distinct purposes.

The entry into the temple is itself of momentous consequence in Luke's Gospel. From the appearance of the angel to Zechariah in the temple (1:5–23) and the prophetic welcome of the child Jesus in the temple by Simeon and Anna (2:22–38), the reader is aware of Jesus' role as "a light for revelation to the Gentiles and for the glory of thy people Israel" and for "the redemption of Jerusalem." Indeed, as Klaus Baltzer has observed, Luke's Jesus came into the temple to take possession of it. With his presence the *kabod* or *doxa* of the Lord is present.[17] But such a visitation was filled with peril as well as assurance. When the purported "liberator" or "redeemer" or divine regent approached any ancient city, no middle ground was possible. Either he was received as "benefactor and savior" and accorded the local traditional acclamations or he was refused at the peril of his wrath. While now working consistently in the medium of royal Jewish traditions, even emphasizing their application by early Christian tradition to Jesus as *king* (19:38), Luke has long since indicated that it is the prophet-king sent by God whose reception or rejection will determine the fate of the city.

The parable of the pounds (Luke 19:11–27), told on the approach to Jerusalem when they "supposed the kingdom of God was to appear immediately," has again alerted the reader to the impending crisis. But this is not a story of eschatological delay (see the parallel in Matt. 25:19 where the master returns "after a long time").[18] Rather, Luke uses the story of the pounds to illustrate the severity of the royal figure whose return in "kingly power" (*labonta tēn basileian*) portends an exacting reckoning for his servants, with judgment and death for those who rejected his rule. The supposition that the kingdom of God was to appear immediately is not addressed directly. But the grim consequences of refusing to acknowledge the dominion of the king are distinctively Lucan features. Whether the dominion of the king actually arrives with his acclamation or his return in power, Luke warns that those who refuse to acknowledge such a king are playing a deadly game and, in effect, are already judged. By introducing this story with a reference to Jerusalem and concluding with Jesus himself "going up to Jerusalem," the evangelist has indicated clearly that the crisis of the drama is at hand.

A literary analysis of the more immediate context reveals the sense of crisis and pathos which has been built into the narrative. The fractured syntax and heaping up of phrases in the passage compounds the effect of Jesus' weeping. In other contexts, Luke has shown that he was fully capable of elegantly balanced and formal Greek prose, and he has demonstrated a familiarity with diverse rhetorical conventions. So his use of a sharply honed future-more-vivid construction may well be calculated to cut to the quick of the apparently modest protest of "certain Pharisees." "Let me tell you, if they are somehow silent, then the stones *will* cry out"[19] (Luke 19:40, author's translation). As in his biting response to the people in Nazareth and to those "certain Pharisees" who bore a warning about Herod, Luke's Jesus has again joined the issue, this time by predicting the dire testimony of the stones: "they will not leave one stone upon another" (19:44); "all the people will stone us" (20:6); "The very stone which the builders rejected has become the head of the corner. Every one who falls on that stone will be broken to pieces" (20:17–18).[20] Such rhetoric is not simply a pathetic fallacy that "the secret of Jesus must out, and if human lips do not confess it, the flints on the road-bed will find a voice."[21] In Luke's narrative, these words render a verdict as severe as that of the king in the "parable": "But as for these enemies of mine, who did not want me to reign over them, bring them here and slay them before me" (19:27). Whatever this logion may have suggested in the time of Jesus or before the destruction of the temple, in the context of Luke's Gospel it expresses bitter irony. In the face of Israel's silence, the stones themselves bear witness, thereby indicting the silence of those who should have joined the chorus.

Luke 19:41–44 must therefore be read first of all as a straightforward and searing oracle of doom, a bill of particulars with an elaborate statement of judgments and sentences.

> If you had known the things that make for peace, all of this could have been averted . . . but since you did not know the time of your visitation, your fate in the days that will come upon you will be as follows:
> 1. And your enemies will cast up a palisade around you
> 2. And they will hem you in on every side
> 3. And they will raze you to the ground
> 4. And your children in you
> 5. And they will not leave stone upon stone in you.
> (Author's paraphrase)

As a *post eventum* interpretation of the destruction of Jerusalem, the retributive force of the oracle marks it as the most explicit "explanation" of that calamity in the New Testament. "Because you did not know the hour of your visitation" stands as the explication of the rejection of the prophet-king, anointed by the Spirit and acclaimed only by the faithful multitude of disciples who do not themselves yet understand his fate. This specifically Christian diagnosis of the point of no return for Jerusalem and the temple must also be acknowledged as *crucial* to Luke's larger theological interpretation. Perhaps it could even be called a theodicy. Since Zechariah first proclaimed that the Lord God of Israel has "visited and redeemed his people" (1:68), even the acceptance or rejection of John was tantamount to "justifying God" or rejecting God's purpose (7:29–30). But still more concretely, the doxological announcement that "God has visited his people" has already been interpreted for the reader as meaning that in Jesus "a great prophet has arisen among us" (7:16). Stephen's account of the rejection of Moses who supposed that his brethren understood that God was giving deliverance by his hand is also cast in terms of their thrusting aside the "visitation" of this prophet saying "Who made you a ruler and a judge over us?" (Acts 7:23–41). The harsh juxtaposition of the suggestion that the disciples be rebuked and Jesus' woeful oracles concerning Jerusalem thus indicates that the "visitation" of the prophet-king who comes in the name of the Lord has already been a proving of Israel. The visitation now spells judgment and destruction for the city instead of the redemption of Jerusalem, or peace, or the immediate appearance of the kingdom (19:11). And why? "Because [*anth hōn*] you did not know the hour of visitation." And if the matter of whose judgment was being exercised is unclear, a review of Luke's use of the term "because" (*anth hōn*) shows it is limited precisely to the renderings of divine judgment (Luke 1:20; 12:3; Acts 12:23).

Yet the thoroughly scriptural coloring and content of these grim words of judgment must be noted once again. As mentioned above, Dodd observed that the oracles are more properly *ex eventu* the destruction under Nebuchadnezzar than the destruction by Rome. Thus Dodd sought to trace their origin back as close to Jesus as possible. But whatever their source, these caustic, ominous words against Jerusalem derive from *within* the Jewish scriptural heritage. They are not uttered de novo against Israel. The entry is a dramatic representation of the great Hallel psalms, emphasizing the entrance of the "king who comes in the name of the Lord." Further, in the fivefold series of oracles defining the impending days, each is filled with echoes of the prophets of old.[22] That "the whole scene of Jesus weeping over Jerusalem could have come straight from the pages of Jeremiah"[23] produces a striking effect, intensifying the rhetoric and pathos by reminiscence of a previous tragedy that is about to be repeated. The reader is thereby led to identify closely with the prophet and his people through the medium of rehearsed authoritative traditions.

Even the phrase "because you did not know" (*anth hōn*) takes on a particular force of divine judgment when it is examined in the light of the use of the same expression by the prophet Jeremiah. The construction is used nine times in the Septuagint translation, and, in every case, rendering the expression simply as "because" may obscure the specific connotation of "this for that." Because Israel has done that, says Jeremiah, the Lord will do this.[24] In only one instance is a positive reward involved: "Ephriam is a beloved son, a pleasing child to me: for because my words are in him, I will surely remember him" (Jer. 38:20,LXX). But in all eight cases where the Septuagint text of Jeremiah used this construction to speak of judgment, it was in reference to the dire fate of the city, the temple, and the exile from the land. Note in particular Jer. 22:8–9: "And nations [*ethnē*] shall pass through this city, and each shall say to his neighbor 'Why has the Lord done this to this great city?' And they shall say, 'Because [*anth hōn*] they forsook the covenant of the Lord our God.'" And 23:38, "Because [*anth hōn*] you have spoken this word, 'The burden of the Lord,' therefore behold, I will seize and dash you down and the city which I gave to you and your fathers. And I will bring upon you an everlasting reproach and everlasting disgrace which shall not be forgotten" (author's translation).

Without attempting to argue for a direct dependence by the evangelist on these specific passages from Jeremiah, Luke's concluding sentence can be clearly recognized as a statement of judgment on Israel which is immersed in the precedent of such specific usage arising from interpretations of the first destruction of Jerusalem. Furthermore, the intensity of the more ancient indictment and the very endlessness of the curse on the city (Jer. 23:40, everlasting reproach and perpetual dishonor) seem remarkably harsh even in comparison with the text of Luke and place such a retributive interpretation of the destruction of Jerusalem within the bounds of Jewish tradition.

The classical prophets provided ample warrant for highly specific identifications of the sin that brought Jerusalem's destruction. Micah could speak of Jerusalem itself as the sin of Judah (1:5) and proclaim its ruin on account of the rulers, priests, and prophets who led it astray into false assurance of divine protection (3:9–12). Jeremiah could emphasize that the desolation of Jerusalem was the prospect for the burning of incense to the queen of heaven (44:22–23; LXX 51). For Ezekiel it was "because [*anth hōn*] you have defiled my sanctuary" (5:11, author's translation; see also 6:11). To be sure, Jeremiah also contended that the prospect of divine visitation could and ultimately would bode for Israel's restoration (see 29:10; 32:41–42; LXX 36; 39): but the "time of visitation" is an awesome and ominous moment of judgment for those who "have healed the wound of my people lightly . . . because [*dia touto*] they did not know [*egnōsan*] their dishonor, they shall fall in their falling and they shall be destroyed in the time of their visitation" (*en kairō episkopēs,* author's translation; 6:14–15; see also 10:15; 11:23; 51(28):18; 48(31):44). This rhetoric concerning the "visitation" as a time of testing and proving for vindication or destruction was still current in Luke's era. It had been transmitted along with accounts of the trials of the elect in the traditions of wisdom, even with specific reference to the testing of the "righteous son of God" (*dikaios huios theou*) whom the ungodly taunt to see if he will be rescued from his adversaries and taken up (*analēmpsetai*: Wisd. of Sol. 2:17–20; 3:7,13; 4:15). Similarly, in the Wisdom of Solomon such ignorance of the secret purposes of God (*egnōsan mustēria theou* 2:21–22) brings judgment and constitutes rebellion against the Lord (3:10).

Luke's peculiar indictment of the ignorance of the "time of visitation" is, therefore, recognizably based on the deuteronomistic prophetic rhetoric of Jeremiah and closely paralleled in available wisdom traditions. In scriptural prophetic traditions, such judgments against Israel could be uncompromisingly harsh. Josephus, Luke's contemporary, could also appeal to such scriptural precedents while going so far as to offer detailed examples of how God intervened on the side of the Romans (e.g., *Wars* 6:399,401,411–12, point of no return 6:322,352). But Luke has not transformed the tradition of Jesus' lament over Jerusalem into a Roman theodicy. It is also misleading to say that in Luke "the destruction is the clear refutation of Judaism."[25] Such a perspective only obscures the vital intra-Jewish hermeneutical argumentation and crisis of national and theological identity that is implicit in this recitation.

Luke's eschatology concerning the destruction may indeed be more prophetic than apocalyptic. The oracles concerning Jerusalem may be couched less in the rhetoric of the abomination of desolation of Daniel, found in Mark, than in the deuteronomistic terms of judgment within history for Israel's unfaithfulness. Still the pathos of the prophet-king Jesus is not unlike that of the Most High and his angels in 2 Baruch: "Dost thou think that there is no anguish to the angels in the presence of the Mighty One, that Zion was so delivered up and that lo! the gentiles boast in their hearts? . . . Dost thou think that in these things the Most High rejoices? Or that his name is glorified?" (67:1–3). No, Luke's Jesus would agree. No comfort can be offered to those Jews or Gentiles who would fail to weep or would justify themselves at the expense of such calamity.

The grounds for this judgment against Jerusalem, although clearly stated, still remain a mystery. If simplistic views of "free will" or "choice" are introduced to interpret the complex issues of agency and responsibility of the text, the same frustration ensues that accompanies attempts to decide in Exodus whether God used Pharaoh to save Israel by hardening his heart or God saved Israel in spite of the fact that Pharaoh hardened his heart. The text repeatedly states it both ways. And even if the theological problem of divine causality was later read into the story of Pharaoh (e.g., the LXX),[26] the tension between apparently contradictory statements concerning Pharaoh's agency resists tidy source-critical solutions. Similarly, Luke's composition defies mere literary, psychological, moral, or even purely theological resolutions of the problem of historical causation, although, finally, theocentric convictions dominate.

Even with the faithful, Luke appears intent on dwelling on their *ignorance* of the course of Jesus' ministry. In the second passion prediction, he prefaces the traditional comment "they were ignorant of this word" (Mark 9:32, author's translation) with a command, "let these words sink into your ears" (see Jer. LXX 9:19, author's translation). Luke also explicates this *ignorance*: "this was hidden from them that they should not perceive it; and they were afraid to ask him about this saying" (Luke 9:44–45, author's translation). The third passion prediction also concludes with a similar triple-sided statement: "Yet they understood none of these things and this saying was hidden from them and they did not know the things which were being said" (18:34, author's translation).

Luke's well-structured disclosure of the fulfillment of the divine plan and *necessity* according to the scriptures (18:31; 24:31,32,35) is thus steadily reinforced by such *ignorance*. The moment "now" when "these things are hidden" (Luke 19:42) stands in a literary contrast with the previous scene where the decisive seeing and not seeing of the one who comes in the name of the Lord (13:35; 19:37–39) had been enacted. And the proclamation of the resurrection will constitute yet another less cryptic occasion for Israel to hear and see what the elect witnesses (see Acts 10:41) have been shown by the risen messiah who opened the scriptures to them. Nevertheless, the problem of why many cannot see, hear, and understand veers between human refusal and divine obscurity up until the citation of Isaiah 6 at the end of Acts, and the "now" of seeing and not seeing continues to afflict Luke's own community.

Even in the sermons in Acts where the apostles proclaim, "let all the house of Israel therefore *know* assuredly" (2:36, emphasis added; see 3:16; 10:36; 13:38), the matter remains painful. The former "ignorance" which produced the tragic consequences of the fulfillment of the scriptures by "those who live in Jerusalem and their rulers" condemning Jesus is forgivable, but still requires repentance (3:17–19; 13:27–41; see also ignorance of Gentiles 17:22–31). The necessity of accountability even for actions and consequences that are apparently beyond human ability to recognize or to anticipate is depicted with care in Luke–Acts.

A comparison with Josephus may once again prove instructive since his theological convictions and historical concern are similar in several respects. When giving an account of a counsel between the Idumeans and the chief priests over strategy in beleaguered Jerusalem, Josephus suggested that "God perverted their judgment so that they devised for their salvation a remedy that was more disastrous than destruction" (*Wars* 4:573). Perhaps such a statement still can be credited with a cold and bitter pity, but little of the prophetic sympathy remains.

Above all, in Luke's presentation of Jesus' grim oracle on arrival in Jerusalem it is the logical incoherence of the passage that marks it as a genuine lament, displaying the pathos of the prophet-king who comes in the name of the Lord. Why are all these calamities to befall Jerusalem? "Because you did not know the time of your visitation." But why? Even the prophet-messiah is at a loss: "If only you knew, even today, the things that make for peace." "How often I have intended to gather you, but you did not so intend" (13:34, author's translation). The matter of a conflict of wills is again focal. The very peace that those certain Pharisees are so intent on preserving as they silence the disciples who proclaim this king will be denied them. Indeed, Luke agrees with Josephus that the tragic irony of the choice that has been made is that it will lead to a greater destruction, and he even allows that the choice is now beyond them: "But now they are hid from your eyes."

But if, like Josephus's, Luke's account is *post eventum* of the destruction, its reticence to pass its own judgment is all the more remarkable. As with the disciples, "who did not know" and "the saying was hid from them," so also for Jerusalem: "now it is hid from your eyes . . . because you did not know." The rejection of the prophet-king does have grim and tragic consequences. Yet this rejection is also tied up with Jesus' mission in his "fulfillment of all the things written through the prophets"—by ascending to Jerusalem (13:22; 18:31).[27] Thus, the mystery of what is the divine purpose which all of this will accomplish is steadily pushed to center stage. Through all the failures and errors of the human agents, in the face of the rejection and because of the acclamation of the prophet-king, what is the plan and purpose of God that this tragic tale displays? Certainly there is more at stake than Josephus's ex post facto justification of God "perverting their minds." Then what is the content of that will? In Luke the grief and anger of Jesus as intensified by the fractured syntax of the passage is specified by the abundance of scriptural phrases and allusions. Love for Israel, conflicting with wrath, characterizes this oracle of judgment.

Until the Times of the Gentiles
Are Fulfilled

Luke 21 has long been a battleground for competing methodologies of interpretation, and it continues to display the inadequacy of prevailing conceptions of the evangelist's enterprise. Both the historicist quest for what Jesus himself said and the redaction critical inquiry for the possible theological significance of the "alteration" of earlier traditions have escalated the search for "sources," but the results of that search are heavily disputed. To be sure, the close parallels in sequence and content which resumed between Luke and Mark in Luke 18 have made the case for the availability of Mark impressively strong. But what of those instances, which increase sharply in chapter 21, where the Markan material was only used with reserve? Must a more fundamental source or document to which Markan materials have now been added be presumed? Or has Mark been thoroughly recast in order that a Lucan concern such as the "delay of the Parousia" may be identified as a clear alteration of Markan eschatology? Or does not this apparent impasse require a reconsideration of the adequacy of the method to the material of the text?[28] Perhaps a more comprehensive view of the evangelist's use of Mark along with available scriptural traditions in the composition of the narrative is indicated.

A literary analysis of this section of Luke would certainly support the view that Luke's composition was more than the transmission of early Christian sources and would challenge highly specific explanations of every alteration. The story itself has integrity. Thus, Norman Petersen's general assessment of the dynamic of Luke's narrative is particularly worth repeating in approaching this section: *"the rejection of God's agents by God's people in connection with God's sanctuaries (synagogue and temple) is the plot device by which the movement of the narrative as a whole is motivated"* (emphasis in the original).[29]

From Jesus' long anticipated entry into the temple when he drives out the sellers (19:45–46), it is his teaching in the temple that provokes conspiracy and intrigue against him. Only the people, "hanging on his words," stand as the obstacle frustrating the determination of the antagonists (19:48; 20:19,26,45; 21:38). For the moment, it is a standoff, a tense interlude when deceitful attempts at entrapment and blistering denunciations of the chief priests, scribes, and elders are staged before the people (19:9–20,26,45–47; 21:1–4).[30] Although ostensibly polite, even the address of Jesus by the opposition as "Teacher" can be as ironic, if not sarcastic, as it is in Mark (20:21,28 //Mark 12:14,19; see Luke 19:39). Yet even the scribes must accord grudging respect for his teaching (20:39–40) and the faithful regard his temple teaching as authoritative (21:7,37). Although Jesus turns back the contrived questions concerning his authority, taxes to Caesar, and the woman widowed seven times, each question still serves as an occasion for genuine instruction for those who are ready to hear, including the denunciations "in the hearing of all the people" (20:45).

Similarly, the comments by some about the adorning stones and offerings prompt Jesus' ominous oracle concerning the spectacle of the "coming days" (21:5–6). Furthermore, the elaborate eschatologically charged paranesis of the rest of the chapter represents Jesus' response to a question concerning apocalyptic timetables and signs which is never answered directly (21:7). Jesus' teachings in the temple are thus not merely foils or corrections of hostile or mistaken questions, but also integral to the plot development. Moreover, the warnings of coming persecutions and of the desolation of Jerusalem all represent an intensified interpretation of the life of the community in the days ahead while carefully distinguishing such perils from the truly apocalyptic end of history when the Son of man is coming in glory (21:8–9,25–27). The present, with all of its difficulty, is the time for witness, endurance, watchfulness, and prayer until the time of the Son of man (21:10,19,36).

The oracle concerning Jerusalem which stands near the crescendo of this temple discourse must also be recognized as part of the literary whole, a painful warning and instruction for the faithful. No delight is taken. Indeed the woe for pregnant and nursing women strikes a note of human pathos in the calamity much like Jesus' counsel to the faithful lamenting women on the way to the crucifixion: "Daughters of Jerusalem, do not weep for me, but weep for yourselves and for your children. . . . For if they do this when the wood is green, what will happen when it is dry?" (23:27–30). No further explanation is supplied of why the destruction will come, except as the phrase "the days of vengeance to fulfill all that is written" recalls the judgment of Jesus' oracle on arrival in Jerusalem. No suggestion is made that the destruction will constitute God's final judgment. In fact, the oracle concludes with the elusive hint of an end to Jerusalem's subjection when "the times of the Gentiles are fulfilled" (21:24).

The comparison of Luke's version of this oracle with that of its probable literary source, Mark, has long generated a wealth of commentary upon Luke's "altered" eschatology. Perhaps the case was stated most succinctly by Georg Braumann. He observed that although the tradition spoke of the Parousia and the destruction of Jerusalem in one breath, Luke separated them *because* he viewed the destruction of the city, which was probably already accomplished, as a consequence of the sin of the city. But Luke anticipated the Parousia as the end of the persecution of the Christian community.[31] To be sure, the words concerning the desolation of Jerusalem under siege convey their own connotation of divine judgment and do not lack eschatological intensity and significance. Yet they are quite distinct from the apocalyptic scenario of the "abomination of desolation" in Mark. Luke's "desolation" is again a theme from the script of the classical prophets who portray God's contention with Israel in judgment and salvation as the subject of history, reserving the promise of the restoration of Israel for the time beyond the tribulation of the present.

The reader who was unaware of Mark's apocalyptic eschatology might well be expected to ponder the ambiguity of this oracle until reading Peter's Pentecost sermon on the text of Joel. There, the community is clearly informed that, in Luke's phrase, the "last days"[32] have already been inaugurated with the exaltation of Jesus as messiah and Lord. In that context, no subtle or intricate midrash is offered, only a direct eschatological application of the text to the time of the community, like a column taken from a scroll of *pesher* exegesis at Qumran: *Pishro*, "This is that!" "This is what was spoken by the prophet Joel" (Acts 2:16).

The Spirit of prophecy has already been poured out, and the blood, fire, and vapor of smoke marking the coming of the day of the Lord must be close at hand (Acts 2:17–21). But if that reader were also acquainted with the passage of Joel which was cited, its status as an oracle concerning the judgment and the restoration of Zion and Jerusalem could not have been missed. Phrases and words elsewhere in Acts 2 also suggest that the author was aware of its force as a proclamation to those "in Jerusalem" offering salvation from the calamity of the city and Mount Zion for those who call on the name of the Lord. Such survivors are identified in Joel as those who are "told the good news" (*euangelizomenoi*), who are those called or chosen by the Lord. Furthermore, the text of Joel immediately proceeds to speak of the "restoration" or "return of the captivity of Judah and Jerusalem" and concomitant judgment upon the Gentiles on account of "my people and my heritage Israel" (LXX, Joel 3:1–4:2).

It is noteworthy that Joel already represents an *intrascriptural* midrash on the prophetic traditions of "restoration."[33] Luke's lectionary of texts concerning restoration is significantly enriched by his later appropriation of Isa. 49:6 and 45:1–22 where the restoration of the scattered of Israel is coupled with its mission to be a light to the Gentiles that "my salvation may reach to the end of the earth." Thus, even the programmatic question and answer of Acts 1:6–8 clothes the expected "restoration of the kingdom to Israel" in the garb of the church's mission in "Jerusalem, Judea, Samaria and to the end of the earth," although the application of this verse from Isaiah to the gentile mission awaits later explication (Acts 13:47). But the "promise" which accompanies the giving of repentance to Israel is not only the gift of the Holy Spirit, forgiveness of sins, and the deliverance from this crooked generation for all whom the Lord calls (Acts 2:39; Joel 3:5), who in turn have called on the name of the Lord (Acts 2:21; Joel 3:5). The promise that accompanies repentance also envisions the beginning of the unfolding of the "times of refreshing" and the restoration of all that God foretold through the prophets (Acts 3:19–21).[34]

In due course, Luke moves on to show how the experience of the community is warranted by the scriptures so that the gift of repentance unto life and of the Holy Spirit are bestowed *even and also* on the Gentiles (10:44,47; 11:17,18; 15:8). Indeed, the text of Amos 9:11–12 is appropriated and enriched with allusions to Isaiah and Jeremiah to maintain that the restoration and rebuilding of the fallen house of David will take place so that "those who remain" may seek the Lord along with "all the Gentiles who are called by my name" (Acts 15:16–18).[35] And it may even be that James's speech in Acts 15 is intended to deal not so much with the matter of the Gentiles per se, because the scriptural warrants for their eventual inclusion were clear. Rather the recitation of Peter's testimony that God *first* (*prōton*) visited the Gentiles is now given a scriptural warrant to demonstrate that even the inclusion of the Gentiles at this unexpected point fits with God's plan to restore Israel: "And with this the words of the prophets agree, as it is written, 'After this [*meta tauta*] I will return, and I will rebuild the dwelling of David.' " God has already equipped himself with "Gentiles who are called by my name" (15: 12–21).

Therefore, the point to be observed in the present discussion is that Joel's apocalyptic schema is invoked intact by Luke *for interpreting the present time* of the "last days" (see Luke 12:56; Acts 2:17). The eschatological drama has begun and awaits its consummation. Neither speculation about God's timetable nor false comfort at the apparent delay may be countenanced.[36]

All of which again demonstrates, on the one hand, that the larger narrative context of a given pericope needs to be adduced along with the synoptic comparisons to estimate the evangelist's investment in a particular episode or oracle. Thus, in Luke 21:20–24 the evangelist has not simply historicized an apocalyptic tradition, but has written the community of his time into the apocalyptic drama at a carefully stated point: "For these are days of vengeance, to fulfil all that is written" (21:22). On the other hand, the previous excursus into Acts also demonstrates again that the particulars of the case can only be recognized by the careful identification of the scriptural grist which the wheels of the narrative were designed to grind. The formal "plot device" only serves to point to the heart of the story. Or to restate the matter in terms of the structure of Luke–Acts, the speeches in Acts will frequently cite or refer overtly to the scriptural texts and motifs thought critical to interpret and explicate issues that are still ambiguous but demonstrably crucial by their literary significance in the gospel.

With reference to the specifics of Luke 21:20–24, moreover, all the prophetic rhetoric concerning the dire fate of Jerusalem resonates with phrasing and terms from Isaiah, Ezekiel, Jeremiah, 1 and 2 Maccabees, and 1 through 4 Kingdoms.[37] Luke also still preserves the dominant scriptural view of the Gentiles as instrumental to God's dealings with Israel.[38] The dire words of "desolation," siege, and flight occasion an eschatological *pesher* or direct application to the times of the community: "For these are days of vengeance, to fulfil all things written." This scriptural motif is further identified by its correlation with the coming "distress" and "wrath" when Jerusalem is trod underfoot by the Gentiles until the times of the Gentiles are fulfilled (vv. 23–24). This subjection and these times of the Gentiles are now viewed in light of the harsh phrase, "days of vengeance."

Such a perspective is entirely credible *within* Jewish scriptural traditions and their contemporary interpretation. The "days of vengeance" was a stock phrase for divine punishment.[39] That ominous threat confronted obdurate Israel repeatedly. In the Septuagint version of Hos. 9:7, the matter was stated most directly: "the days of vengeance have come, the days of your retribution have come and Israel shall be afflicted." This verdict was also specifically applied to the destruction of Israel for unfaithfulness in forsaking God.

The image of Jerusalem trod underfoot by the Gentiles was also recognizable as a scriptural motif reminiscent of Zech. 12:3 (LXX): "and in that day I will set Jerusalem as a stone trod under foot [*katapatoumenon*] by all the Gentiles." In 1 Maccabees 3 the wasting of Jerusalem and the trampling of the sanctuary by the Gentiles evokes fasting and repentance: "And they opened the book of the law to inquire into those matters about which the Gentiles were consulting the images of their idols" (v. 48). And in 2 Baruch 67, the black eleventh waters, "the calamity which is now befalling Zion," produce the anguish of the taunt of the Gentiles who "assemble before their idols and say, 'She is trodden down who often trod down.'" The reproof of Israel is fundamental to all of these passages, and no warrant would exist in such traditions for suggesting that the "times of the Gentiles" could be anything but a cause of remorse.

It is worth noting, at least by way of contrast, that in Mark 13:10 the proclamation of the gospel to the Gentiles had itself been assigned a position in the unfolding apocalyptic agenda. Had Luke picked up Mark's insistence that "First the gospel must be preached to the Gentiles," then his view of the "times of the Gentiles" would have appeared in a more positive light. Furthermore, Luke's presentation of Paul's parting remark to the Jews in Rome might then have been seen as more than a standard Jewish-prophetic reproof for unfaithful Israel: "Let it be known to you then that this salvation of God has been sent to the Gentiles; they will listen" (Acts 28:28). But Luke's silence at this point (21:13) leaves no option but to recognize that no interest has been expressed in the Gentiles themselves in Luke 21. All of the references to the wars (v. 10) and distress of the nations (v. 25) and the times when they tread down Jerusalem are focused upon interpreting the situation of Israel in the midst of the days of vengeance.[40]

It must also be noted, however, that those same passages which present the triumph of the times of the Gentiles as instrumental to God's dealing with Israel consistently present *divine vengeance* as leading to *divine vindication*. Thus Zech. 12:3, 1 Macc. 3, and 2 Baruch 67 all regard the treading down of Jerusalem by the Gentiles as punishment which is but preliminary to the vindication of God's name and justice. Just when the Gentiles tread on Jerusalem and begin to take pride in the triumph of their role over the God of Israel, they stumble. The days of *vengeance* against unfaithful Israel anticipate the days of *vindication* of God in which Israel is restored: "Then all the Gentiles will know that there is one who redeems and saves Israel" (1 Macc. 4:11). "At that time after a little interval Zion will again be builded, and its offerings will again be restored, and the priests will return to their ministry and also the Gentiles will come to glorify it" (2 Baruch 68).[41] The same *vengeance* that requires the *vindication* of God's faithfulness at the expense of an unfaithful people also produces the *vindication* of the people called by God's name in the presence of the Gentiles.

Perhaps nowhere is this dynamic more thoroughly developed than in Deuteronomy 32, the Song of Moses, previously identified as a crucial available scriptural resource for the interpretation of Israel's history according to the deuteronomistic pattern of apostasy, punishment, and vindication.[42] Along with the avenging which Deut. 18:19 promises for all who do not "hear" the words that the prophet like Moses speaks, the divine vengeance/vindication announced in Moses' predictive history of Israel gave rise to diverse specific interpretations. Yet the assurance was as clear as the threat. In the face of all the punishments for Israel, "a perverse generation, children in whom [there] is no faithfulness" (Deut. 32:20; see Ezekiel 20; Luke 9:41; Acts 2:40), only the pride of the foolish nations used by God to provoke Israel prevents the final dissolution of Israel and its memory. Lest the foolish nations say, "Our hand is triumphant, the Lord has not done all these things," the vengeance/vindication of God turns into the vindication of the people of God: "in the day of vengeance, I will repay . . . for the Lord will vindicate his people [*krinei*] . . . see, see that I am [*egō eimi*] and there is no God but me" (Deut. 32:35,36,39, author's translation).

Luke does not cite these traditions directly in this passage, nor is it possible to prove conscious or explicit allusions to specific scriptural contexts. The traditional association between threat and promise is thoroughly assimilated into the narrative itself. Only the connection between the cryptic phrases concerning the "days of vengeance" and "the times of the Gentiles" as scriptural fulfillment is offered to indicate the frame of reference. The specific connotations which the evangelist assumes these ciphers will evoke can only be approximated now by the identification of similarly loaded terminology in extant literature related to comparable occasions. The vital synagogue debates and discussions concerning these days of vengeance/vindication and the times of the Gentiles that most probably lie behind the text can also only be estimated.

Yet reading Luke 21:20–24 within this frame of reference makes the intra-Jewish character of the discussion inescapable. "These days of vengeance" which fulfill the scriptures are Luke's present times, *the times to be interpreted*. These are not yet the times of the restoration of the kingdom to Israel (Acts 1:6) nor of the final apocalyptic disclosures associated with the coming of the Son of man (Luke 17:20–37; 21:25–36).[43] These are the "times of the Gentiles" during which Jerusalem, "trod down by the Gentiles," still awaits God's vindication of his people when the "times of the Gentiles" will be fulfilled. Now is the time to watch and pray (21:36), to observe the signs of healing and restoration that have already been disclosed,[44] and to await the fulfillment of all of the scriptural promises. The times and seasons of such fulfillment may still be obscure to human knowledge. But in spite of the dire fate of Jerusalem and the severe reproof it represents, it has not even been considered that the Gentiles have replaced Israel or that God's long-standing promises to Israel will fail to be fulfilled.

Luke's other usages of the term vengeance/vindication (*ekdikēsis*) also reinforce such a reading of this oracle concerning Jerusalem. Perhaps it is fortuitous that in Acts 7:23–29 it is Moses who "defends" and "vindicates" one of his brothers among the sons of Israel from abuse by the Egyptians. Perhaps. But it is surely significant to the exemplary value of that story that such vindication was to be understood as divine deliverance and yet was misunderstood as only threat.

Furthermore, in the story of the persistent widow in Luke 18:1–8, the expectation of the vindication of the "elect of God" is full of hope. In an extreme comparison intended to show that "so much the more" than the unrighteous judge will God vindicate his people, the question is only, "How long?" The story is introduced with the standard eschatological counsel to pray and not lose heart (see 21:36) and concludes with the correlation of the speedy vindication with the coming of the Son of man. Thus, the "delay" which is being discussed is not merely the "delay of the Parousia," but it is the interval when the suffering of the people of God at the hands of their adversaries, perhaps even as divine punishment, awaits divine vindication.[45]

In the end, therefore, even the dire fate of Jerusalem still awaits further fulfillment in Luke's expectation. The punishment for not "knowing the time of your visitation" by the prophet-messiah is severe. These are the times of the Gentiles and the days of divine vengeance. But the day of the Son of man, the fulfillment of the times of the Gentiles, and the restoration of the kingdom to Israel will not fail. This is the time for the elect of God to pray always, not to lose heart, and to cry to God day and night in anticipation of vindication (18:1–8). Now when the city probably lies in ruins and the reader locates the time of the church *within* this unfolding apocalyptic drama, a crucial aspect of *interpreting the present times* is the continued watchfulness, preparedness, and expectation that even the delay is only a sign of divine forbearance, enabling repentance.[46] Such restraint is not to be scored or presumed upon.[47] Divine vengeance is awesome in its proportion and exaction. Yet even God's wrath or punishment is an assurance, for its force is not simply vengeful toward the people or vindictive toward evil. Rather this *vengeance* is finally perceived as the *vindication* of both the justice and faithfulness of God. Since God's promises to the people still await fulfillment, even the "days of vengeance" are already a sign of the awaited day of divine vindication of the faithful when the Son of man will be manifest to all.

4

The Messiah Must Die

The Definite Plan and
Foreknowledge of God

If the rejection of Jesus, the anointed prophet-king, required interpretation and if the subsequent destruction of Jerusalem and the temple could threaten the hope that Jesus signaled the fulfillment of God's promises to Israel, then the crucifixion of the messiah by the Romans was all the more problematic: "a stumbling block to Jews and a folly to Gentiles" (see 1 Cor. 1:23). The matter was not simply academic nor original with Luke. The practical difficulty of heralding the reign of a messiah for Israel was inescapable for early Jewish Christians, since most Jews did not acknowledge Jesus in such a role either before the destruction when the kingdom of Israel was already in great peril or after the temple and city had been devastated. The dissolution of the nation marked by the slaughter and dispersal of the people, the loss of the common religious sites of holy city and temple, and the consequent impulse to reconstitute a purified people preserved from the taint of unfaithfulness preoccupied all surviving forms of Jewish faith and life. The threat of the total destruction of whatever social, political, and religious cohesion still remained compelled the formation of more fixed or normative traditions, hastening the division of the church from the synagogue, the sharpening of the gentile question, and even the "propagation of one, universally recognized text form" of the scriptures.[1] Thus, in an era when the common ground between the messianists and other Jewish

97

groups, most notably the Pharisees, was rapidly slipping away, Luke was apparently under a particular obligation to confront the problem of Jesus' execution, since he testified to God's continuing relationship with Israel in *vengeance* and *vindication* as the fulfillment of scriptural prophecy.

Modern Christian readers have had an extremely difficult time recognizing the distinctive Lucan interpretation of Jesus' death as occasioned by such historical circumstances and hermeneutical debates. Indeed, at the risk of presumption, it may be helpful to identify some of the methodological, theological, and historical considerations that have often both obscured Luke's distinctive contribution and disclosed something of its peculiarity.

Approaching Luke as a redaction of Mark, for example, has exposed the contrast between Mark's theology of the cross, with its cosmic expiatory significance, and Luke's more schematic presentation of God's saving purpose and actions in history. Thus, when the extent of and intra-Jewish character of the non-Markan materials in Luke's passion narrative were made evident, especially as correlated with the speeches in Acts, Luke's Christology was often characterized as "pre-Pauline"; therefore, the cross represents only a misunderstanding of the Jews which God must remedy with the resurrection.[2] Or, for those who found such thoroughly Jewish argument incredible for the evangelist himself, these materials appeared to support Luke's use of a Proto-Luke document to which Markan additions had been made, although the magnitude of that hypothetical document began to rival Luke–Acts itself.[3] The method of evaluating Luke's narrative as a redaction of sources, therefore, unveiled its peculiarity but tended to interpret that distinctiveness in terms dictated by earlier Christian sources.

Studies seeking to assess Luke's view of the significance of the death of the messiah have recognized the evangelist's singular emphasis on its necessity, but they have often limited their descriptions to a contrast with a view of satisfactory atonement and spiritual forgiveness ostensibly drawn from Paul. Thus, it is argued that "as strongly as Luke asserts that 'the messiah must suffer,' he draws no inner redemptive or atoning significance from this fact." Therefore, the cross serves no intrinsic salvific purpose, so that it is soteriologically empty of meaning except as part of the whole plan of salvation. Whereas, Paul, for example, sees God decisively at work in the events of cross and resurrection Luke finds God at work only in the latter. The hour of the passion belongs to men, who are in effect set in opposition to God's will.[4]

The modern gentile Christian aversion to "nationalistic" understandings of Jesus as liberator of Israel, whose reign promised a restoration of the kingdom, has certainly caused Luke to suffer further by comparison with Paul.[5]

The dominance in Luke's theology of the resurrection–assumption as the vindication of Jesus' death[6] may also tend to reinforce the view that the offense of the death has been removed or absorbed by the exaltation of Jesus as messiah and Lord. While neither Paul nor Mark will allow any neglect of the cross, Luke's many affirmations concerning the *necessity* of the passion may finally not exempt him from the charge of having composed a pious martyrdom, which is but the unfortunate prerequisite for exaltation: "a temporary reverse which is speedily retrieved by Jesus' resurrection."[7] Again, for many later gentile Christian readers, the wonder of the resurrection may itself be such a telling demonstration of divine approval that the scandal of a crucified messiah is already overcome.

But no such easy evasion of the cross was possible for this evangelist. In fact, Luke further elaborated the Markan traditions concerning the *necessity* of the suffering of the Son of man as being in accord with the scriptures (Luke 9:22//Mark 8:31; Luke 9:44//Mark 9:31; Luke 18:31//Mark 10:33; Luke 22:22//Mark 14:21; Luke 24:7). He also repeatedly stressed that the suffering of the messiah was warranted by the scriptures and was therefore *necessary to the divine plan* (Luke 24:26,46; Acts 3:18; 17:3; 26:23).

Perhaps the force of such appeals to the scriptures can best be estimated by recognizing that Jewish tradition had learned to be cautious even about the demonstrative value of spectacular displays. Paul told the Galatians that "even if we or an angel from heaven should preach to you a gospel contrary to that which we preached to you, let him be accursed" and proceeded to ground his argument concerning circumcision in the scriptures. In a famous rabbinic story from a later era, Rabbi Eliezer is supported in his argument on a disputed point by a voice from heaven (*Bath Qōl*), to which Rabbi Yehoshua replied definitively by quoting Deut. 30:12: "It is not in heaven." The story continues:

> What did Yehoshua mean by saying, "It is not in heaven"? Rabbi Yeremiah explained: "Since the Torah has already been given from Mount Sinai, we do not pay heed any longer to a heavenly voice. You yourself, O Lord, wrote in the Torah given at Mount Sinai: 'Turn aside after the multitude.'" And God cries out in heaven, "My sons have defeated me."[8]

And if this episode appears too far removed from the immediate discussion of demonstrations, Luke's conclusion to the story of the rich man and Lazarus puts the matter more succinctly: "If they do not hear Moses and the prophets, neither will they be convinced if some one should rise from the dead" (Luke 16:31). The scriptural warrant for the suffering and death of the messiah was at least equally crucial to authenticating the accomplishment of God's saving purposes as the testimony or proof of the resurrection.

The *opening of the scriptures* by the risen Lord was also fundamental to the revelation of the resurrection itself. As Paul Schubert observed,

> Luke's indifference to the "point" of the traditional story of the empty tomb, and his indirect admission that even appearances by themselves can be explained away, are in his view completely robbed of their force by the assurance that the attested events of the life, death, and resurrection of Jesus as the Christ are guaranteed beyond doubt, by the long-foretold and on-going prophecies which unfold in history the "will and plan" of God[9] (see Acts 2:23; 4:28; 13:36; 20:27)

Yet no explicit scriptural citation is offered to warrant the affirmation that it was *necessary* for the messiah to suffer. Only general appeals to the scriptures are offered: "Moses and all the prophets" (24:27), "everything written about me in the law of Moses and the prophets and psalms" (24:44), the "mouth of all the prophets" (Acts 3:18), arguing from "the scriptures" (Acts 17:2–3), and "what the prophets and Moses said" (Acts 26:22). This lack of specific scriptural warrant becomes all the more conspicuous when a subsequent combing of the material leads to the apparent conclusion that "nowhere is it even intimated that the messiah should suffer, neither in the Bible as written nor in the Bible as read in first century Judaism."[10]

As has been indicated above, Luke does adduce specific scriptural texts to document Jesus as the prophet like Moses, signal the eschatological moment of Pentecost, and diagnose the lack of hearing in Israel. By contrast, therefore, the very generality of the appeals for scriptural warrant for the suffering of the messiah suggests an awareness that a different mode of argumentation was required. Having identified Jesus in terms of Moses the prophet, ruler, and liberator of Israel, and of David the king, prophet, and servant, he not only drew upon a wide range of traditions concerning the suffering prophet but focused the presentation with a few crucial allusions and citations from Isaiah's depiction of the chosen servant who suffers. Yet it is very doubtful that a "suffering servant concept" as such can be assumed, although Isa. 53:7–8 does provide significant resources for the proclamation of the good news of Jesus (Acts 8:26–40). Nor does Luke draw upon Isaiah 53 to develop a concept of Jesus' death as expiatory. In fact, he appears to neglect precisely those features in the text.[11]

Further study of the way in which Luke's narrative is informed and legitimized by the scriptures is clearly required, and a few suggestions will be made in the last section of this chapter. But instead of describing what the author is *not* doing in comparisons with Mark or Paul or contrasts offered by modern criticism of the "suffering servant songs," one should evaluate Luke's mode of argumentation from the scriptures in its own right so far as possible. Nor will it prove adequate to label his use of the scriptures as "atomistic" or as a "proof from prophecy"[12] unless the effort is pursued further to identify what was at stake and what kind of "salvation" this crucified Jesus whom God exalted as messiah and Lord was to have accomplished.

In fact, crucial as the titles "messiah" and "Lord" were to anticipating Jesus' role in the extended prologue (see especially 2:36; Leader and Savior 5:31), the lack of a specific proof text for a suffering messiah does not present an insuperable obstacle. Instead, the force of the argument is cumulative and apparently self-conscious in

101

its retrospection on Jesus' ministry and death.[13] The argument is further corroborated by appeals to Jesus' fulfillment of Davidic psalms, such as those concerning the gathering together of the Gentiles and the peoples of Israel against the Lord's anointed (Acts 4: 25–28; Psalm 2) and the preservation of the "holy one" from corruption (Acts 2:25–28; 13:35; Psalm 16). Acts indicates repeatedly that the case to be argued from the scriptures is that Jesus is the messiah (see especially 5:42; 9:22; 17:3; 18:5,28; and Luke 23:35), and the premise that the messiah must suffer was crucial to that case.[14] Nevertheless, the larger picture of the "will and plan of God" as disclosed in Moses, all the prophets, and the psalms is the overriding concern. The more specific discussion of the messianic proof serves the evangelist's prevailing interest in interpreting all "the things which have been accomplished among us" (1:1) as consistent with the will and plan of God.

Given the persistence of the question of Jesus' messiahship and Luke's assurance that "the holy and sure blessings of David" are bestowed on Jesus (Acts 13:34), it may well be that the narrative is offering a response to disturbing hermeneutical objections raised from within or without the Christian community. How can a crucified Galilean be identified as God's anointed ruler? Where are the manifestations of the fulfillment of those Davidic promises? Such questions did not find obvious answers in the late first century A.D. Thus, even the stories of personal salvation and healings brought by Jesus and the apostles are never far removed from being signs portending the eschatological reign of God inaugurated by this "anointed" Jesus.

Nevertheless, these concerns are taken up in the framework of a larger theological concern. The net of scriptural warrants is much broader than a specifically "Christological" controversy. It gathers up traditions of the pathos and suffering of the prophet, especially the prophet like Moses, along with expectations of divine restoration of the royal Davidic line. It links them through the vocabulary of the servant of God, including the servant who suffers, and correlates them to traditional stories of Jesus' career as anointed prophet, ruler, savior, servant, and king.

The argument is thus decidedly circular. The most crucial proof that the messiah must suffer may even be that Jesus, in whom all the scriptures are fulfilled, suffered. Since the promises of a servant-prophet and servant-messiah both came to fulfillment in the one Jesus, clearly the messiah also had to suffer for *"everything* written about me in the law of Moses and the prophets and the psalms must be fulfilled" (Luke 24:44, emphasis added). The answer may precede the question. But in the face of a chaotic and contested history, even this effort to speak of the divine will and plan must be acknowledged as testimony to the faithfulness of God. The stated objective of proving that Jesus and the beginnings of the church are the fulfillment of the scriptures is never far removed from the larger and more painful task of demonstrating that the present times are within the divine economy and that God's promises to chosen Israel will not fail to be fulfilled.

Luke's Tragic Narrative of the Passion

Luke's narration of the speeches of Peter and Paul to Israel in Acts probably offer the most explanatory commentary conceivable on his passion narrative. The indictment seems painfully direct: "Let all the house of Israel therefore know assuredly that God has made him both Lord and Christ, this Jesus whom you crucified . . . whom you delivered up and denied in the presence of Pilate, when he had decided to release him" (2:36; 3:13–15; 4:27; 7:52; 10:39). Yet in the address to the "brethren and sons of the family of Abraham and the god fearers" (Acts 13), in which Paul diagnoses the events, something of the human tragedy also comes into view: "For those who live in Jerusalem and their rulers, because they did not recognize him nor understand the utterances of the prophets . . . fulfilled these by condemning him."[15] Even that qualification of the indictment still only touches the surface of the human pathos and divine mystery of the passion narrative itself. No tidy explanation of the details of the story can come to grips with the profound drama of the contention between human and divine wills and the wonder of a divine triumph on behalf of the people in the midst of the human tragedy of rejection, misunderstanding, and failure of nerve that drives the story forward. Thus, before turning to the hermeneutical agenda implicit in certain aspects of Luke's treatment of the harsh realities of Jesus' death, some description of the sweep of the passion narrative is required.

The story of the betrayal, trial, and execution of Jesus in Luke

22–23 is also the story of the people. No modern literary sense of character development or exploration of psychosocial motives can legitimately be found, but the evangelist does appear capable of exploring the interaction between the set groups and figures so that the role and plight of diverse characters can be perceived in some detail. Once again, the formal medium of Greek tragedy, especially as mediated by the tragic historians of the Greco-Roman era, comes to mind. Furthermore, as in the tragedies, actions or even unspoken words may provide clues to the human predicament in the face of the powers that apparently or actually determine the course of events. Such disclosures are often figurative or ambiguous; they are more mysteries to be pondered than actions or choices to be explained.

A thorough analysis of the whole of Luke–Acts in comparison with first-century popular tragic drama and tragic-rhetorical histories would be a profitable study in itself, but even to suggest the general paradigm requires an initial observation. That is, Jesus is not a tragic hero in this passion narrative. As early in the narrative as the transfiguration story, if not the sermon in Nazareth or the childhood appearance in the temple, Jesus knows about the *exodus* which he is to fulfill in Jerusalem. This is quite unlike Greek drama in which the content of the final scene or *exodus* is obscure to the tragic figure during the development of the plot.[16] Indeed, Jesus' full awareness of what his rejection as prophet-messiah portends and his complete obedience to God's will (see Luke 22:46) anticipate his suffering, not because he has defied God or has been forced to violate the law of Israel or Rome. Rather he endures the passion in faithful obedience to his vocation as prophet-messiah. "He dies not because he has sinned, but because he has not sinned."[17] In this light, Luke's theocentric story belongs more in the Jewish scriptural tradition of contemplating the wonder of God's awesome yet intentionally gracious involvement with the people than in the tradition of Greek tragedy, where the plight of the human agent is the primary subject.[18]

But the people and the disciples who intend to remain faithful are presented in a manner which highlights the tragic consequences of their actions as they are caught up in a drama they are unable to comprehend. The bitter tears of Peter (22:62), the laments of the women (23:27), and the beating of the breasts by the multitudes

(23:48) all represent Luke's tragic vision of a people swept along in a current of intrigue and betrayal as they recognize the inevitable consequences of their participation too late to alter them (23:49). Perhaps the most poignant commentary of all, which once again transforms this story into an interpretation of the times of Jerusalem's destruction, is offered by Jesus on the way to his execution:

> Daughters of Jerusalem, do not weep for me, but weep for your-selves and for your children. For behold, the days are coming when they will say, "Blessed are the barren, and the wombs that never bore, and the breasts that never gave suck!" Then they will begin to say to the mountains, "Fall on us"; and to the hills, "Cover us." For if they do this when the wood is green, what will happen when it is dry? (23:28–31)

Even the faithful women and their yet unborn children have been caught in a web which is not of their own weaving. Perhaps the evangelist was borrowing a convention from the repertoire of contemporary tragic poets or from the historians' pathos-filled rhetoric of siege-warfare in order to enrich with notes of human anguish his story of what God has accomplished through Jesus. The archaic traditions which give this narrative its particular force must still be identified by means of the scriptural phrasing that permeates the story; but now, as applied to the human situation, this is the stuff of which tragedy is made.

The primary agents and cultic setting of this brief and dramatic story are all presented with an economy of words. Then the antagonists quickly join forces in a collusive intrigue of betrayal (22:1–6). The determination to put Jesus to death has already been made, and the only question to be debated is "How?" Nevertheless, the roles assigned to the several groups of figures in the story are carefully differentiated.

The chief priests, the scribes, and the rulers have been set in direct opposition to Jesus since the time of his entry and lament ("Would that even today you knew the things that make for peace"), followed immediately by the cleansing of the temple, commencing Jesus' daily teaching in it (19:41–47). While the Pharisees disappear from the narrative at that point, the antagonistic chief priests, scribes, and principal men lack only the means to destroy him. Consequently, all of Luke 20 focuses on a series of encounters with this religious leadership in which Jesus proves to be more than a match for their trick questions and attempts at entrapment. Refusing to respond to a leading inquiry concerning John's baptism, Jesus first turns the question around and then tells the grim parable of the vineyard, which the scribes and chief priests perceive to be directed against them. Having been set up by spies of the chief priests and scribes who in feigned sincerity raised a question concerning tribute to Caesar, Jesus' nonanswer leaves them silent again (20:7,26) since it left open the judgment of what belongs to Caesar and what to God. Then the preposterous case presented by certain Sadducees to ridicule belief in the resurrection is transformed by Jesus into a scriptural argument for the resurrection, reducing the question to its absurdity. Even the scribes, who probably stood with the Pharisees and the messianists on this question, must commend his answer and dare ask him no more. Thus, Jesus' hermeneutical question concerning the messiah as David's son and lord not only anticipates its explication in Acts 2 by means of the resurrection but further exposes the ignorance of the scribes. Their condemnation, which concludes the chapter, is thereby intensified.

Jesus' teaching of the people in the temple therefore takes place in prospect of the awesome threat of which he is fully aware. But the antagonists cannot accomplish their will on their own. Specifically, the people who cling to Jesus' words, the faithful in Israel who gladly hear his teaching in the temple, frustrate the malevolent plans of the antagonists (19:48; 20:19,26,40,45; 21:38; 22:1,6; see also 11:53–12:3). As at the beginning of his ministry when the Devil departed without success "until an opportune time" (*kairos* 4:13), Jesus now appears invulnerable.

But it is then that Satan "entered" one of the twelve. Now a collusion of forces, demonic, political, religious, and apostate, is able to mount a feasible plan for "how" and "when" (*to pōs, eukairia* 22:4,6) he might be betrayed "in the absence of the multitude." In time, even the people and the disciples who represent faithful Israel will participate in the denial of Jesus if not in his betrayal. Yet the anticipation of the interlude of the passover meal is intensified for the reader by

106

the knowledge that only Jesus and his adversaries are aware of the malevolent plot against him.

Perhaps *Judas* could have been portrayed as a tragic figure in the story. His sin occasions the action and produces his own destruction as well as that of Jesus. Certainly Jesus' oracle concerning him, which is common in the synoptic tradition, has often been read to support such a view: "For the Son of man goes as it has been determined [Matthew and Mark: "As it is written of him"]; but woe to that man by whom he is betrayed" (22:22//Mark 14:21//Matt. 26:24). But in Luke–Acts, Judas's own motivation is never explained (see Matt. 26:6–16; John 12:1–8; 6:70–71; 13:27). Jesus' word to him is only indirect (see Matt. 26:20–25; John 13:21–30; Luke 22:21–22). Judas's role in the arrest is reported with minimal elaboration (22:47) and he is never presented as having "seen" or otherwise acknowledged his sin (see Matt. 27:3–10, *hēmarton*). Acts merely reports that "this man bought a field with the reward of his wickedness" and died a gruesome death (1:18), no doubt implying divine judgment (see Acts 2:15–20; 12:20–23). In short, there is no tragic dimension to his character. The Son of man is the one whose course is *determined,* not Judas. But Judas is still held accountable as the man through whom he is betrayed. Nor does the report that Satan "entered" him alter his active apostasy in which he "departs" and "confers" with those in league with the power of darkness (22:3–6,53).[19]

Peter, by contrast, is at least pathetic if not tragic in Luke's account. Whether Judas, Peter, or anyone else except Jesus act of their "free will" in the story is extremely doubtful, and even Jesus has submitted his will to God's (22:42). But Peter's denial is followed by immediate remorse upon remembering the word of the Lord (22:54–62). Still, the agency of Satan, though indicating that the struggle transcends mere choice (22:31–34), does not exempt Peter from culpability for his lack of faithful confession.

A great deal has been written about the possibility that Luke's passion narrative offers a pro-Roman apology at the expense of the Jews. Many of the arguments advanced are weighty, especially if the assumption of a non-Jewish community context of the work is left unchallenged. But the clear effort to locate responsibility for a Roman execution within Israel is fully consistent with the evangelist's interest to interpret Jesus' birth, ministry, rejection, death, and exaltation *within* the framework of the scriptural prophecies to Israel. Like the prophets of old, he only deals with the great imperial forces from *within,* even when Roman officials and functionaries express complete disinterest in denominational Jewish disputes over "words and names and your own law" (see Acts 18:12–16; 19:33–34; 22:30–23:16; 24:22–27; 25:13–22; 26:24–32). Although Luke acknowledges the actual domination of Rome, he persists in the view that the destiny of Israel and its messiah is not determined by external forces except as these are instrumental to God's purposes. The course of history is to be plotted in the interaction between the purposes of God and their reception or rejection by a willful people.

Certainly Luke is intent on exonerating Jesus and his followers of all charges and on demonstrating that they were no threat to the Roman order. Such an "apology" would have been vital to the self-understanding of the Christians even if no Roman officials ever bothered to burrow through such strange sectarian literature, and the threefold verdict of Jesus' innocence by Pilate (Luke 23:4,16,22) would serve such apologetic interests. But even those interpreters who regard Luke as attempting to clear Pilate of Jesus' death must concede:

> If Luke's apologetic was addressed to some Roman official on behalf of the church, then his presentation of the trial of Jesus would only raise more questions than it answers with regard to the relationship of Roman justice to the Christian church. Why was Pilate so superficial in his investigation of the serious charges against a suspected rebel? Jesus was not even "examined by torture." If Jesus really was innocent, why did Pilate not insure his protection? Why would Pilate, charged with thoroughly and fairly administering Roman justice allow this trial to be turned into a lynching?[20]

Pilate's antics certainly would earn him no high marks in Roman jurisprudence! Even if Luke's depiction of him seems kind in comparison with what is known from Josephus about his arbitrary cruelty and disrespect for Jewish customs, it is still very difficult to credit Luke's Pilate with integrity. Again, compared to the presentation in Matthew and John, the figure of Pilate is only minimally sketched in Luke. The report that Pilate had mingled the blood of the Galileans with their sacrifices (13:1) has already revealed his cruelty—an instrument of divine wrath. So now he appears to be carried along by the whim of the crowd. The difficulty he has resisting the charges of sedition which could implicate him (see John 19:12) does not excuse his perversion of justice (Luke 23:23–25). Nor does the bizarre friendship formed with Herod through this event serve as a commendation. Herod has previously been identified as the evildoer who shut John in prison, the executioner of John who wanted to see Jesus, and the "fox" who reportedly wanted to kill Jesus (3:19; 9:7–19; 13:31–32). His curiosity and the mocking of Jesus for a sign only display the absurdity of his court. Long ago, Jesus had indicated that the threats of Pilate and Herod (13:31–32) would not determine his course; rather they would be instrumental to it.

Both *Herod* and *Pilate* are, therefore, only plot functionaries. Nevertheless, they are also accountable for their complicity. Perhaps the gruesome account of the death of Herod Agrippa, who attacked the church and was proclaimed a god, can be viewed as the kind of divine punishment that would be appropriate for such rulers as it was for Judas.[21] But their fate need not preoccupy the narrative, since they are presented only in service of the dramatic interaction of God's messiah-prophet, Jesus, with the rulers of Israel, the disciples, and the people. So also, in the speeches of Acts, the initiative of those in Jerusalem and their rulers is stressed to such a degree that Pilate, while not exonerated, is rendered almost inconsequential (3:13; 13:28). Such a view is not only astonishing historically but it also represents a vision of how God contends with Israel. By contrast, Josephus reports himself standing outside of besieged Jerusalem and counseling surrender on the grounds that the universe is subject to the Romans since fortune has passed to them and God now rests in Italy (*Wars* 5:366–67,378).

Pilate's and Herod's roles in the story, however, are given a peculiar significance based on the corresponding agenda of Psalm 2 concerning the gathering together of the kings of the earth and rulers with the Gentiles and the peoples against the Lord and the Lord's messiah (Acts 4:25–28). That scriptural warrant alone would be sufficient to establish that Luke regarded Pilate and Herod as culpable along with the rest, even if the travesty of quadruple jeopardy at the hands of a judge who lacked the will to follow his clear verdicts was not so obvious. But the citation of Psalm 2 also indicates that for Luke neither the whims of the judges, the antagonism of the rulers, nor even the vacillation of the people finally determines the drama.[22] In the midst of all the intrigue and compromise of justice, all of these agents were gathered to do whatever God's "hand and . . . plan had predestined to take place" (Acts 4:28). Consequently, when Luke reports that Pilate acceded to their demand and "Jesus he delivered up to their will" (Luke 23:24–25), the question of whose will is actually being done has only been sharpened ironically.

The existence of genuine and active opposition to God's will is never denied in Luke–Acts, nor is such opposition absorbed by a divine determinism or transported into a cosmic struggle. Jesus' conscious obedience to the divine will (22:42) also allows him to recognize the magnitude of the opposition. Not only are the chief priests, captains of the temple and elders identified, but they are given their grim due which acknowledges their alliance with the "power of darkness," that is, Satan (22:52–53; see Acts 26:18). Again and again in Acts, the culpability of Israel and especially the rulers is announced (see especially 3:17; 4:8–11; 5:27–30; 6:15–7:1; 13:27).

The very intensity of these indictments, particularly as focused upon the leaders and the self-serving, places Luke within the prophetic stream flowing from Deuteronomy through contemporary wisdom literature. Moreover, Luke's harsh depiction of their antagonism still does not match the severity of the indictments of (false) prophets, priests, princes, and shepherds of Israel pronounced by the prophets Jeremiah and Ezekiel in view of the first destruction and exile. Nor does it compare with the picture Josephus paints of the deceit, intrigue, and vicious greed of the parties vying for power within besieged Jerusalem. In the wake of the actual calamities and divisions within war-torn Israel, Luke's vision of both God's vindication and Israel's unfaithfulness may seem very severe coming from someone who identified with the Jewish nation. And yet the spirit of his harshest accusations and boldest assurances harks back to 1 Baruch: "And you shall say, 'Righteousness belongs to the Lord our God, but confusion of face, as at this day, to us, to the men of Judah, to the inhabitants of Jerusalem, and to our kings and our princes and our prophets and our fathers, because we have sinned before the Lord' " (1:15–17).

Even Luke's characterization of the antagonism of the rulers is not without relief. Whether or not the textually difficult word from the cross, "Father, forgive them; for they know not what they do" (23: 34), was in Luke's original narrative, it nonetheless corresponds well with the judgment that the rulers and the people were acting in *ignorance* (Acts 3:13; 13:27). Furthermore, even within the council, Luke alerts the reader to Joseph from the Judean city of Arimathea "a good and righteous man, who had not consented to their purpose and deed . . . he was looking for the kingdom of God" (23:50–56; see also Gamaliel in Acts 5). From Simeon and Anna to Joseph and the disciples on the way to Emmaus after the resurrection, the faithful in Israel never gave up hope in their expectation of "the consolation of Israel" (2:25), "the redemption of Jerusalem" (2:38), "the kingdom of God" (23:51), the "[redeeming of] Israel" (24:21), and the "[restoring of] the kingdom to Israel" (Acts 1:6). Such expectation of faithful Israel was found even among the wealthy rulers.

But the pathos of the story that most closely approximates tragedy lies in the plight of the people. Indeed, perhaps the most telling sign that Luke–Acts was written by someone who was closely sympathetic with Israel is the sensitive treatment given to the compromised role that the people play in the passion narrative.[23] This account was not composed as a gentile "apology" at Israel's expense.

While consistently accepting the deuteronomistic-prophetic view of human responsibility, Luke's characterization of the people resists any simplistic, moralistic view of choices and consequences. It portrays their actions and words against the background of the accomplishment of inscrutable and incomprehensible divine purposes through means of even the most hostile and blind human agents. To draw an analogy from an earlier post-destruction debate, Luke's theodicy turns out to be closer to Job's vision of the dominion of God than to the moral or theological recriminations of Job's friends and comforters.

Having been thoroughly alerted to the obstacle that faithful people present to the forces that plot to destroy him (19:48; 20:19,26, 40,45; 21:38; 22:6), the reader may well expect that the people's

111

(*laos, ochlos, plēthos*) role will be carefully delineated in what follows. And since the betrayal was designed to take place in the absence of the multitude (*ater ochlou* 22:6), it is crucial to note that the multitude that comes to arrest him (*ochlos* Luke 22: 47//Mark 14:53//Matt. 26:47) has been carefully identified: "the chief priests and captains of the temple and elders, who had come out against him" (v. 52). This "multitude" must not be confused with the crowds of the people! Similarly, the crowd (*plēthos*) that brings Jesus before Pilate is specified: "the elders of the people . . . , both chief priests and scribes" (22:66; 23:1). Consequently, first Peter is trapped in the courtyard of the high priest at night and becomes involved in the denial of Jesus in spite of his best intentions (22:54–62), and then the antagonists move through the Sanhedrin trial and on to the court of Pilate *before* the people reappear on the scene. The plot thickens in the dark of night and those who would defend Jesus are themselves put on the defensive. The ploy to arrest Jesus in the absence of the multitude has effectively compromised his protection by the faithful people. Now, in the light of day, the people's role of advocacy and support has also been compromised.

Luke's version of the charges lodged against Jesus is replete with irony and vicious sarcasm easily recognized by the reader as deceitful. Yet even the misconstrued geographical summary of his ministry serves as a fitting counterpart to the geographical outline of Acts 1:8, so that the composing hand of the evangelist is readily detected. The errors of misinterpretation are obvious, but the high priests and Pilate give voice to the evangelist's point of view (Luke 23:2–5).

It is not entirely clear exactly when "the people" reappear. It is obvious, however, that after Pilate has addressed the high priests and the crowds, those who respond are Jesus' adversaries, who simultaneously implicate "the people" with the very charges laid against Jesus. The verdict by the Sanhedrin is a fait accompli, and any defense that might be offered by the "people" for this "disturber of the nation," now charged with forbidding tribute to Caesar and seditious confusion of the people, would only demonstrate the truth of the charge and place the people themselves in grave jeopardy with no apparent benefit to Jesus. Placed within the oppressive political climate of Pilate's procuratorship, the double bind of the people is as perilous as Peter's entrapment in the courtyard of the high priest.

By the time Pilate has dispatched Jesus to Herod's court for further public spectacle and denunciation by the chief priests and scribes (23:10), "the people" who are called together by Pilate along with the "chief priests and the rulers" (23:13) are now further pressed by Pilate's pronouncement that he plans to release Jesus (vv. 13–16). Whether that suggestion is feigned, intentionally inflammatory, or sincere may be impossible to determine and even beside the point. However, the thought that Pilate was only baiting the Jews to evoke further denunciation of Jesus is both historically credible and conceivable within the irony of Luke's account. In the final interchange (vv. 20–24 where the participle *thelōn* is probably causal and should be read to express Pilate's actual intention to release Jesus rather than Barabbas, v. 20), it would appear that even Pilate is carried along willy-nilly in the torrent. Not even the release of a genuine insurrectionist and murderer can be prevented, and the charade generated by the trumped-up charges against Jesus has gotten out of control. In any case, like Peter, the people are now clearly included, whether by cooption or volition, among those who loudly demand that he should be crucified (23:13,18,21,23).[24] So the ultimate bizarre turn in the grim story has Pilate yielding to the demand of the mob and releasing his own prisoner: "but Jesus he delivered up to their will" (vv. 24–25; see Acts 3:14).

This scene is historically incomprehensible and painfully ironic for the reader who possesses privileged knowledge concerning the divine will which will be vindicated in the face of such willful yet involuntary human actions. The human pathos is also intensified since immediately upon leaving Pilate's court the people appear in a changed role. Their complicity in this execution by their urgent denunciations is already firmly established, as will be reaffirmed repeatedly in the speeches in Acts. But like Peter who denied Jesus three times with increasing vehemence in the high priest's courtyard and then wept bitterly, so also after the third and final denunciation of Jesus before Pilate, in which the people had displayed increasing adamance, the great multitude of the people, particularly the women, immediately began to wail and lament. And Jesus' oracle minces no words over the dire fate of Jerusalem as a result of this act.

Along with the women, the rest of the people are no longer crying out against Jesus nor are they actively engaged in the execution. The indefinite "they" who led him away and seized Simon of Cyrene (v. 26) and who came to the place called the Skull, crucified him (v. 33), and cast lots (v. 34) are probably the Roman soldiers of verse 36, although the silence about their identity is deafening. The scoffing by the rulers (v. 35) emphasizes their continuing active participation. Now, for their part, the multitude of the people only follow Jesus, and at the site of the execution, the people (*laos*) merely "stood by watching" (v. 35). As in the days prior to the terrible moments in Pilate's court, Israel is again divided. Even the two criminals are caught up in an argument with each other concerning Jesus and the kingdom (vv. 39–43).

Literarily, the human drama that surrounds the cross is perhaps as fascinating as Jesus' death itself and points to the disclosure of that more profound mystery. The reader who has been informed along the way to anticipate the outcome and its significance is also given *insight* through the eyes of the onlookers, who thus serve much as a chorus in a Greek tragedy. Furthermore, having seen Peter's repentance for his threefold denial and having been informed that at least part of the "multitude of the people" has already grasped the tragedy of Jesus' situation as well as their own, the reader can hardly resist observing the people who are watching the execution for some signal of significance. Since all the sarcastic mockery of the rulers and soldiers and the railing of the criminal is ironically the truth, the fascination of the spectacle is intense. As W. C. Greene says of Greek tragedy:

> . . . a deeper irony is to be found where all the characters fail to perceive the significance of a saying, or the inevitable outcome of a course of action which is apparent to the spectators, who share the privileged position of the poet and of the gods, and who moreover already know the essentials of the myth. We and the gods, as it were, are omniscient, and share the intimacy of a secret knowledge; we see all and hear all that goes on, and behold men inadvertently and blindly walking toward their doom.[25]

The moment of recognition is identified with great precision. Twice Luke uses the vocabulary of *watching,* portraying the people as *spectators* who had come to see the *spectacle* (*theōrōn* v. 35, *theōria* v. 48), *without* indicating what the people were perceiving. The scorn of the soldiers, rulers, and criminal hangs in the balance against the lone testimony of the innocence of Jesus and the expectation of his kingdom by the penitent thief until, to the accompaniment of cosmic and cultic portents, Jesus heralds his death as a submission to God and expires. And the next word is *idōn*: "upon seeing" or "because he saw what had taken place." Maximizing the dramatic effect and specifying the instant of disclosure, the moment of Jesus' death is the immediate past occasion appropriated by the second aorist participle.[26] "When Jesus had said this, he expired. *Upon seeing* the event the centurion glorified God by saying, 'Truly the man, this one, was innocent' " (*dikaios,* author's translation; see Acts 3:14; 7:52). Then a pun on the stem for spectacle/sight/seeing/insight further defines the insight of the crowds who had gathered for the *spectacle (theōria):* "when they had *seen* [*theōrēsantes*] the things that had taken place, beating their breasts they turned back" (*hupostrephon*). Meanwhile, in an outer ring stand *all* Jesus' acquaintances and the women who had followed him faithfully from Galilee "in order to *see* [*horōsai*] these things" (emphasis added, author's translation).

Exactly what all of these observers are perceiving in the spectacle may still be obscure. Clearly the eyes of the centurion have been opened so that the reader can benefit from his doxology for the righteous one. Yet he is such a cipher in the story that his word is like an oracle. It is impossible to tell if he was only a spokesman for justice or if he is to be credited with deeper knowledge or even if he spoke "of his own accord."[27] Similarly, the lamentation of the on-looking crowds who had now *seen* takes on added significance for the reader. Perhaps their *turning* even suggests that repentance is already underway.[28] Yet all the followers who behold the spectacle and Joseph of Arimathea who awaits the kingdom of God are strangely silent about what they behold. In retrospect or from the vantage point of the reader, their silent presence may well be an eloquent testimony to the constancy and endurance of the faithful in Israel who looked for the kingdom. But for the moment, only the tragic complicity of *all* the *personae dramatis* in this grave injustice is disclosed publicly: "Clearly this man was innocent!" The harsh verdict recapitulates Wisd. 4:16: "The righteous man [*dikaios*] who has died will condemn the ungodly who are living."

115

Seeing is everything in the narrative, and hearing causes scales to fall from the eyes (see Acts 9:17–18; 22:13; 26:12–19). But the *tragic vision* of human complicity, whether intentional or involuntary, only leads to the darkness of despair or remorse. Indeed, *insight* may be granted through the most unlikely spokesman, such as the centurion in the synoptics. Or in Josephus's account of the Jewish war there is the obscure peasant who abruptly cried out ("as if moved by a demon") against the temple and the city.[29] Or again, the scene in Sophocles's drama of Oedipus the King comes to mind, in which the herdsman, about to divulge the terrible secret of Oedipus's origins, hesitates, saying, "O God, I am on the brink of frightful speech." To this Oedipus replies, "And I of frightful hearing. But I must hear." So with the truth divulged, the remorse of the *insight* of the tragic figure causes his blindness.

> O,O,O they will all come,
> all come out clearly! Light of the sun, let me
> look upon you no more after today!
> I who first saw the light bred of a match
> accursed, and accursed in my living
> with them I lived with, cursed in my killing.[30]

This is not to suggest that Luke had read Sophocles or even Josephus. The avenues through which such basic conventions of tragic literature might have been conveyed to the evangelist within or without Jewish circles are diverse: rhetorical historiography, national romance literature, and the biographies or martyrdoms of illustrious heroes and philosophers. At any rate, like many of his contemporaries who shared training in rhetoric, the evangelist displayed considerable competence in the art of communicating pathetic and tragic effect through stylistic devices and the structuring of the narrative plot.

Luke's distinctive view of the tragic plight of the people, however, does further reinforce the argument for his close identification with Israel. Historically incredible as the neglect of the Romans in this story is and politically unrealistic as the picture of Pilate may be, viewing the destiny of Israel from within the bounds of faithfulness or apostasy to God's purposes is common to a wide spectrum of contemporary Jewish interpretations of Israel's situation. Although

Roman disinterest and disdain for Jewish denominational squabbles is acknowledged in Acts (see 18:12–17; 25:22–27), it is still *intra-Jewish* party strife that carries the Romans along in service of Paul's vocation to go to Rome (21:11; 15–25:12). Luke is persuaded that "the things that have been accomplished among us," especially the rejection and exaltation of the prophet-messiah, have not only "not been done in a corner" but have actually determined the course of history. That same grand vision of Israel's election requires an intense assessment of Israel's own responsibility for its plight in an era of grim realities, as other Jewish interpretations of the times in terms of the scriptural heritage agree. Through neither a hatred of Israel nor a self-denigration of a people, but because he was possessed of that *vision* of Israel's election, the evangelist must conclude in chorus with those traditions that the fault is not in our stars nor in the power of Rome, but in ourselves and our unfaithfulness to God.

Yet Luke's well-crafted story of the passion also anticipates further *insight*. As the continued play on the vocabulary of *seeing* and *recognition* in Luke 24 indicates, there is more to be seen in what has transpired than is apparent. Thus, the resurrection appearance of Jesus on the Emmaus road (24:13–35) suggests two disciples are discussing recent events, but when Jesus joins them they are unable to *recognize* him (v. 16, see vv. 23–24). Their inability to *recognize* Jesus provides occasion for a lesson by him in scriptural interpretation concerning the connection between the suffering of the messiah and his exaltation into dominion (vv. 26–27). Then, in the course of breaking bread together, "their eyes were *opened* and they *recognized* him." After he disappeared, they further interpret their recognition: "Did not our hearts burn within us while he talked to us on the road, while he *opened* to us the scriptures?" (vv. 31–32, emphasis added).

From the vantage point of the people, the passion narrative is indeed tragic, filled with destructive ignorance and belated insight. But even on the level of the story, it is clear that the tragedy is transcended. The resurrection does not obliterate the passion or turn it into a taunt of Israel, but it requires a reexamination of the passion in the light of the scriptures. Tragic as it is, the narrative is more than a testimony to the blindly ignorant complicity of Israel with the forces of darkness. In fact, it furnishes a theocentric commentary on Israel's

117

history and distress. It is finally a story of the vindication of God's reign through his servant messiah, proclaiming the giving of repentance unto forgiveness to Israel and even to the Gentiles, and anticipating its full disclosure when "the times of the Gentiles are fulfilled" (Luke 21:24). Once again, the story leads beyond the problem of human sinfulness without false assurances or blanket condemnations and even beyond a preoccupation with tidy moralistic theodicies. It sets the whole account within a *vision* of the counsels of God, which vast and inscrutable though they be, are nevertheless also faithful to God's declared intentions for Israel and the Gentiles.

This Is the King of the Jews!

The scriptural resources that have been appropriated to narrate the story of the passion are so extensive that the riddle as to which elements are historical and which are midrashic is almost completely unsolvable.[31] In addition to the discussion in the first section of this chapter concerning the lack of explicit scriptural warrant for the proposition "the messiah must die," a few examples should be selected to demonstrate how the scriptural allusions and coloring of the narrative constitute and define a theological or theocentric commentary on the tragic tale of Jesus, which is also the story of a suffering people. To put the matter simply, for the reader who was privy to the intense hermeneutical discussions of the Jewish scriptures with reference to Jesus and the times, the story did not trivialize the human pathos but it did supply the scriptural clues for the *insight*: "God has not deserted the people after all!"

It must be granted, moreover, that the historical myopia of modern readers still requires the complex and sophisticated optics of historical-critical exegesis to identify moves made with scriptural resources that seemed quite natural and appropriate to ancient interpreters. And even when the way such groups as the covenanters at Qumran read themselves into the eschatological agenda of prophetic texts by means of *pesher* exegesis has been recognized, this approach does not commend itself to many as an attractive hermeneutical model for current appropriation of the scriptures.[32] Or, to alter the metaphor, the problem is that of listening at the keyhole of the texts to an elaborate hermeneutical discussion, now conducted in the sophisticated medium of the story of Jesus' death. Moreover, that discussion took place in a social, ethnic, political, and religious context far removed from the context of the modern interpreter and can only be overheard in an alien tongue across a gap of almost two thousand years, during which time the material has almost consistently been used against the Jewish people. And only a limited portion of this enclave exegesis is still audible through the extant text.

All of which is but a prelude to the observation that a literary analysis of Luke's composition may produce a picture of the "making of Luke–Acts" that is actually a mirror image, reversing the sequence of the historical process. Thus, the reading of Luke–Acts may be enhanced by the observation that Luke has constructed this two-volume work by seeding the narrative of the Gospel with scriptural language and complex allusions, which are then harvested in the explicit scriptural arguments in Acts and in accord with the hermeneutical warrants of Luke 24. This observation may even provide another sign that the evangelist has managed the literary skills of thinking a book through backward. But it must not be allowed to belie the fact that the same hermeneutical discussions and debates depicted in Acts also preceded the writing of Luke's gospel narrative in the experience of Christian readers.

Luke's tantalizing reference in the prologue to the many [who] have undertaken to compile a narrative (1:1) would already be a signal of an *inter-Christian* discussion of "what has been fulfilled among us" even if the literary links with Mark and Matthew had not preoccupied a century of gospel studies. Furthermore, the coherence of the synoptic Gospels is itself testimony to the relative stability of those traditions about Jesus, especially as anchored in the sayings of Jesus and narratives of the passion.[33] The constraints of discrete traditional modes of correlating the story of Jesus with the scriptures and the disciplined transmission of community memories further guarded against uncontrolled fictionalizing of the story. But Luke's narrative also manifests the adaptability of these living traditions by its dramatic remodeling of gospel sources, confident marshaling of diverse materials from "all of the scriptures," and thorough restaging of the speeches in Acts to parade a cast of authoritative spokesmen for credibly familiar yet recognizably Lucan views. The objective of now identifying the "point originally scored," in any such recital of tradition, therefore, requires that the literary composition be assessed in close connection with the hermeneutical options and resources available to the evangelist.[34]

Luke's depiction of the plight of the people thus appears in a new light. Crucial as the literary description proved to be for documenting the close identification by the evangelist with the people, and perhaps startling as that identification may be to modern gentile readers, it was not a contested point in the text. Certainly the neglect of the Romans, the parallels with Peter's denial, and the tragic *vision* of a people trapped in their own complicity are signs of careful attention to the human pathos of the story, and one of the marks of the genius of narratives is their ability to carry several points. Yet the tragic remorse of the disciples and the people is in no way turned into a glorification of the Romans or a vindictive mockery of the Jews for the fate of Jerusalem. Nor is it an assignment of blame to the Romans. The remorse and conviction at the word "this man was innocent" is itself a sign of the recognition of the need for repentance. The intra-Jewish context of the narrative and its consequences is simply assumed.

The literary elaboration of the tragic blindness and convicting *insight* of the people does, however, point toward the heart of an issue that plagues Luke's vision and requires interpretation. "The rejection of God's prophets by God's people" is more than a plot device which evokes associations from contemporary tragic literature and more than a technique for testifying to divine providence. As the book of Acts displays so clearly, this rejection also represented a continuing existential threat to the community's assurance that the reign of God had indeed been inaugurated by the anointed Jesus. The question of the identity of true Israel in "the present times" was tied up with a hermeneutical crisis as reflected in competing interpretations of the correspondence or lack of correspondence between the scriptures and the life of the people. Instead of the gathering of Israel to shining Jerusalem followed by the humbling of the Gentiles, Jerusalem's doom at the hands of the Gentiles and even the inclusion of Gentiles ahead of many in Israel were being proclaimed as integral to the reign of the crucified messiah. The question of why all of Israel does not *recognize* Jesus as messiah was not merely a literary or hermeneutical device and certainly not a polemical justification of gentile Christianity at the expense of the Jews. The very assurance of "the things accomplished among us" (Luke 1:1) was at stake, and the scriptural basis for interpreting this rejection within the times and seasons of God's promises and plan for Israel was crucial. Indeed, the death of Jesus, the destruction of Jerusalem, and the rejection of Christian preaching were three mysteries of a cry requiring scriptural interpretation, and they all came to expression in the passion story.

The issue is sharpened in Acts by the several accounts of the rejection of Christian preaching, where such rejection was usually also accompanied by considerable acceptance by Jews. In three instances (13:46; 18:6; 28:28) the clear reproof for such rejection is the turning to the Gentiles. Since the last instance includes the additional rejoinder that the Gentiles "will listen" and it sets the tone for the last episode in the books of Acts, many commentators have concluded that the rejection of the Jews is thus complete and the gentile mission is founded on the failure of the Jewish mission.[35]

But prophetic reproofs of Israel are so much a part of the rhetorical baggage of the tradition that it would be very unlikely that they would suddenly be taken so literally. After the first two such parting salvos, Paul and Barnabas are soon back in Jewish synagogues (13:46–14:1; 18:6–19). Nor does Luke proceed to depict the Christian mission among Gentiles as an unqualified demonstration of "hearing." Even in Acts 28 where the narrative trails off quickly, several details militate against any view that "Luke has written the Jews off."[36] First, Luke states explicitly in that context that "some were convinced by what he said, while others disbelieved" (v. 24). At the least, Acts concludes with a divided Israel. Second, although the manuscript evidence for verse 29 is very weak, it indicates that at least some ancient scribes understood that the dispute among the Jews was far from over. But the third and most crucial point is that the passage appropriated from Isaiah which diagnoses this disbelief as obduracy is a classic prophetic refrain. The refrain borders between condemnation for "this people" (i.e., God's people) and assurance that even the rejection of the prophet's word by such a "rebellious house" (see Ezek

12:2) can be part of the alien work of God. It also appears from the targums that these verses from Isaiah were understood within certain circles of Israel in Luke's era as prophetic prevention not only of the healing but even of the forgiveness of Israel.[37]

Yet there is no cause to assume that even such harsh judgments imply an end of the Jewish mission or the justification of the gentile mission at the expense of the Jews. A more modest suggestion might be that Luke is turning a strenuous objection against the inclusion of Gentiles into an argument that such inclusion represents divine intervention to reprove the nonmessianists or more strictly observant messianists for "withstanding God" (see Acts 5:39; 11:17; 15:14; compare Romans 9–11). The rift between those Jews who believe Jesus to be the light to the Gentiles and the glory of Israel and those who do not is profound, and both sides have fortified their positions with scriptural arguments. Yet all of Luke's allusions to the redemption of Jerusalem and the restoration of the kingdom suggest that he was also aware that Isaiah's oracle further envisioned an end to the grim days. For after "cities lie waste" and "the land is utterly desolate," Israel is to be reconstituted through a surviving minority (Isa. 6:11–13).

At any rate, upon returning to the problem of the tragic blindness and belated insights of the people and the disciples in the passion narrative, the literary observation is dramatically specified by this hermeneutical discussion (see also Luke 8:10b; 10:23–24). As with the watching and close observation of Jesus in Nazareth followed by rejection, the fact that a scripture is fulfilled "in your ears" does not mean that it will be heard, or that the people will listen to the prophet like Moses, or that those who watch intently will see (Luke 4:14–30; Acts 3:22–23). And if those who do not listen are "destroyed from the people" (Acts 3:23), that does not mean that the people will be destroyed or that God has abandoned the promises made to Israel.

But Luke does regard the *ignorance* or blindness of Israel as constituting culpability and requiring repentance. By means of the word of the apostles' preaching and the deed of the healing of the lame man, which are to be heard and seen (see Acts 2:22,37; 3:12; 4:13), it is *made known* to Israel that the Jesus "whom you crucified" has been exalted as Lord and messiah (2:36; 4:10).

Again, a helpful comparison can be made with Josephus's account of his own speech delivered to the residents of besieged Jerusalem from a safe distance outside (*Wars* 5:375–419). Josephus also called for Israel's confession and repentance while pleading for those who dwell in Jerusalem *to hear and recognize* that they were withstanding not only the Romans but God as well. Josephus's recitation of Israel's history was also a *post eventum* literary composition. But the final appeal of this address to Jerusalem offers a diagnosis in terms of the blessings and curses of Moses (401; see Deuteronomy 32) which probes the fallen carcass of the besieged populace for "secret sins" that will now be exposed (402,413–14). "Nevertheless," Josephus continues, "a way of salvation is still left for you, if you are *willing* [*ean thelēte*], and the Deity is placable to those who confess and repent" (415).

Granting the practical wisdom of Josephus's eloquent speech as vindicated by his hindsight on the destruction, its human and theological obscenity can still not be disguised. The exoneration of the speaker, the glorification of the conqueror, and the humiliation and demoralization of the vanquished are all stock features of the vicious oratory of siege warfare. In Josephus, however, God's will and Roman might are all but equated: "To scorn meaner masters might, indeed, be legitimate, but not those to whom the universe was subject" (366). The cruel challenge, "if you are willing," offered now in retrospect of the inability of all but a few to choose to desist from the rebellion, only further burdens the victims while seeking to relieve this Jewish author and his Roman compatriots. And finally the content of this "confession and repentance" is merely the surrender of arms to the Romans with pathetic appeals for the preservation of the glory of the city and pleas of pity for the children, wife, and parents "ere long to be the victims either of famine or of war" (416–19).

Luke's appeal for repentance, however, is of a very different spirit, caught up with the plight of the people: "Would that even today you knew the things that make for peace! But now they are hid from your eyes" (Luke 19:42). Luke is confident that even as the messiah-prophet was rejected and executed by Israel in accord with scriptural predictions, God's exaltation of the crucified Jesus as messiah and Lord was not merely a reproof of Israel and a demand for submission but a gracious offer of repentance unto forgiveness and unto life for Israel and the Gentiles (Luke 24:46–47; Acts 2:32–39; 3:13–21; 5:31; 10:42–43; 11:18; 13:26–39). Even the vision or hearing that touches the heart is already a sign of the continuing divine intention to bestow the promises on Israel (Acts 2:37–39).

Consequently, for those blessed with "eyes to see and ears to hear . . . the things accomplished among us," the deeper mystery of God's providence is also disclosed. The tragic plight of Israel swept under by the forces of ignorance and darkness is not ignored. Yet, finally, no mere faceless fortune or malevolent power has been served by the death of the messiah or the destruction of Jerusalem. Nor is "the will and plan of God" only an abstract assertion. Rather, as the scriptural clues which are woven into the tapestry of the entire narrative are identified, they display the fulfillment of divine promises. The content of that will and plan is finally the salvation of the people.

That "the messiah must die" is demonstrated more by the accumulation of diverse traditions than by systematic argumentation. What is implicit in the scriptural correspondences will be explicated through postresurrection hermeneutics in the speeches in Acts. But in the passion narrative, the drama is choreographed to gather up all the scriptural resources possible. Even the episode of the two swords is apparently rehearsed to show explicitly that "it is necessary that what is written be fulfilled in me" (Luke 22:37; Isa. 53:12, author's translation).

The suffering of the righteous prophet and servant of God like Moses comes together in Luke's presentation of Jesus along with the acclamation of the royal messiah and servant of God who is son of David. Finally, the anointed prophet-king, heralded at Jesus' presentation in the temple and proclaimed in the words of Isaiah in the synagogue at Nazareth, is publicly announced by the rulers of Israel as God's messiah and chosen one. The sarcasm of those rulers does not diminish the insight for the reader, since at the transfiguration Moses and Elijah had indicated that he was to accomplish his *exodus* in Jerusalem and the voice from heaven had linked Jesus' royal role as Son of God to that of the chosen servant of Isaiah. He was the one to be "heard" (Luke 9:28–36; see also 9:51 *analēmpsis*; 12:50 *baptisma*). The explicit citations of Isaiah 53 (22:37; Acts 8:32–33), the frequent references to the servant roles, and the pronouncement of Jesus' innocence may even suggest that this mode of speaking about Jesus provided the locus around which the specifically royal and prophetic vocabulary could cluster. Thus, it is as the chosen one, the servant of God, that this Jesus the messiah suffers and fulfills all the scriptures.[38]

Yet the taunt of the Romans preserved by all the Gospels and emphatically underscored by Luke's syntax furnishes the last word: "The king of the Jews is this one!" (Luke 23:38, author's translation). The ultimate irony is that in their mockery both the rulers of Israel and the Gentiles do herald the truth that transcends the tragedy: "Behold, you scoffers, and wonder, and perish, for I do a deed in your days, a deed you will never believe, if one declares it to you" (Acts 13:41; Hab. 1:5). This Jesus, enthroned in ignominy, is indeed the one who through his obedience to God's will is enthroned as messiah and Lord. He is the light to lighten the Gentiles, and the glory of Israel, God's people, and the hope of Israel's restoration is lodged in him. As disclosed in the vindication of his death in resurrection and assumption, he is the messiah of God, his chosen one: "The king of the Jews is this one!"

5

Fear Not, Little Flock

When a prophetic word is spoken is as much a criterion of its validity in scriptural traditions as *what* is said. Whether the announcement is an appropriate application of the authoritative tradition to the situation is crucial for testing the spirit that has inspired the prophecy. Not that the classical prophets could ever be domesticated to polite society, but their speech and behavior, which often seemed outrageous, were later judged to have been the only appropriate and faithful response to self-assured or oppressive communities intent on self-preservation. Thus, Luke's recitation of Jesus' invective against the people in Nazareth has been judged as a prophetic critique. Like the scriptural prophets, Jesus has read aliens and outcasts into the eschatological drama, thereby reproving the constitutive interpretation of Isaiah 61 by which the religiously respectable people garnered those promises for themselves.

Perhaps no blasphemy is quite like that of a prophetic critique that is no longer appropriate to the situation or that falls into the hands of outsiders. There is a time when saying, "Peace, Peace!" is a lie and a delusion (Jer. 6:14). Again, there is a time when nothing will suffice but to say, "Comfort, comfort my people, says your God. Speak tenderly to Jerusalem, and cry to her that her warfare is ended, that her iniquity is pardoned" (Isa. 40:1–2). And there is also a time when even in the midst of the chaos and recriminations of the aftermath of a tragedy with "men fainting with fear and with foreboding of what is coming on the world," that the prophet's oracle reassures:

"look up and raise your heads, because your redemption is drawing near" (Luke 21:25–27). Even afflicting the afflicted may be unavoidable during the time that the stern alternatives for diagnosing human culpability in a disaster are still being fought out on the basis of the scriptures. But when such traditional prophetic rhetoric is later made absolute in the detached self-understanding of a new community, the prophet's sympathy, investment, and identity with the people may be perverted into a cruel self-justification at their expense.

The matter is of consequence for the interpretation of Luke–Acts, if for no other reason than that from the second century to the twentieth most of its expositors have read this narrative at the expense of "the Jews," frequently with little or no concern and perhaps with disdain for the obvious evidence of the struggle within the Jewish context from which it originates. Luke's pastoral assurances of the continuity of the faith and his missionary charges have often been misappropriated as warrants for some of the most triumphal and imperialistic religious-political schemes imaginable. His affirmation of divine providence has been used to construct a theology of history to confirm oppressive dogmas of manifest destiny, racial superiority, and class struggle, as well as a host of personalistic schemes of "God's plan for your life." With the ascendancy of gentile Christianity and the virtual disappearance of Jewish believers in Jesus as messiah and Lord, generations of gentile Christians have often ignored their dependence on the faith of Israel and boasted of their faith over against "the Jews," neglecting both the story of Luke–Acts and the direct counsel to the Gentiles of Paul (Romans 11). The prophetic critique has become constitutive or self-justifying and the assurance of the continuity of divine promises to the elect has been turned into a doctrine of Christian progress with the replacement of "old" Israel.

This analysis of the literary and hermeneutical agenda of Luke–Acts within its probable historical setting certainly need not be beyond dispute in all of its points to challenge such misuse of the work. Perhaps, for example, a more credible case may yet be made for a prewar date of composition, but that would probably only press the origins of Luke–Acts closer to a Jewish Christian context and compound the mystery of the oracles concerning Jerusalem. Again, even if it could be demonstrated conclusively that the author was or was not a circumcised son of the covenant, the close identification with the people and high investment which Luke made to show that myriads of Christian believers were faithful, observant Jews would still remain. Furthermore, all the obscure hermeneutical arguments and appeals to experience are employed to resolve the question of the status of the Gentiles inclusively even if their inclusion appeared to be "out of sequence" according to prevailing interpretations of the scriptures. Perhaps such scriptural hermeneutics might still serve as a lesson for those who, on the basis of their reading of Luke–Acts, seem to have all the phases of the divine plan figured out, especially the exclusion of "the Jews."

But the more the historical occasion of the work can be identified in terms of the struggles surrounding Israel in the last third of the first century A.D., the more clear it becomes that the prophetic stance is also taken firmly within Luke's own community. The prophetic oracle is still vital in a community which identifies itself strictly on the basis of God's vocation and election of Israel. The bold assurances of divine providence and of the continuity of God's saving activity in and through Israel, now extended to the Gentiles, are offered in the face of devastating discontinuities. The parity and congeniality among Jewish and gentile Christians leave the church vulnerable from within and without to charges of apostasy and "going the way of the Gentiles" at the very moment when the future of the faithful observance of the Torah was in jeopardy. Furthermore, the lack of public vindication of the prophet-messiah Jesus in a time when Jerusalem itself was at least doomed and probably destroyed further sharpened the issue of true and false prophecy. Indeed, the times demanded that any assurance that would be offered must come to terms with the harsh realities of a divided and defeated Israel, especially if the reign of the King of the Jews was to be heralded as the inauguration of the eschatological dominion of God.

It is one thing for the Roman poets and historians to credit mighty *Fortuna* and their own virtue for the ascendancy of the empire while their imperial armies proclaim, "God is on our side." But it is quite another thing for those who are oppressed to trace out a correlation between their present experience and their historic faith. As with contemporary nationalistic romance literature in which dominated peoples exalted the mighty deeds of their ancient national heroes to endure their subjection with dignity,[1] some extravagance in the portraits of the wisdom and powers of the founding messiah and his apostles could even be expected in Luke's narrative. Yet the grand style of the Lucan prologue and the synchronistic correlations with the reigns of emperors, kings, high priests, procurators, and governors still do not disguise the harsh realities: harassment, imprisonment, scorn, and execution. Nor can Luke's literary artistry and theocentric critique of the rhetoric of the "benefactors" obscure the fact that his twin works belong to the literature of the vanquished, not to that of the dominant culture.

The time for the prophet Jeremiah to purchase land in Jerusalem and to promise a new covenant reportedly came when "the army of the king of Babylon was besieging Jerusalem, and Jeremiah the prophet was shut up in the court of the guard" (Jeremiah 32). Similarly, the time to compose a "narrative of the things accomplished among us" (Luke 1:1) came when the "divine plan" for salvation history was anything but obvious. Perhaps Luke's theocentric assurance may even be a most crucial sign of the community distress which it intends to assuage.[2]

The mystery of election, therefore, now threatens to pit the vanquished against each other, with all parties striving for a renewed faithfulness or righteousness. However, this agonizing quest for faithfulness is not simply a matter of denominational theological differences. The identity and survival of a people are bound up in the assurance and peril of having been chosen by God. Under extreme pressure, the adequacy of every effort to refine and integrate the authoritative tradition into an *interpretation of the times* is severely tested. Second Baruch may plead:

> And let us not now look unto the delights of the gentiles in the present, but let us remember what has been promised to us in the end. For the ends of the times and of the seasons and whatsoever is with them shall assuredly pass by together. The consummation, moreover, of the age shall then show the might of its ruler, when all things come to judgment. (83:5–6)

Fourth Ezra may lament

> And now, O Lord, behold these nations which are reputed as nothing lord it over us and crush us. But we, thy people whom thou

hast called thy first-born, thy only-begotten, thy beloved most dear, are given into their hands. If the world has indeed been created for our sakes, why do we not enter into possession of our world? How long shall this endure? (6:57–59)[3]

And for his part, Luke may affirm that now the times of the Gentiles and the restoration of all await their fulfillment, and the knowledge of the times and seasons belongs to God alone. Even now, the exalted messiah is present through his Spirit, Name, and apostles to offer repentance unto forgiveness to Israel and even to the Gentiles.[4] Nevertheless, the longing for the "restoration of the kingdom to Israel" is keenly felt: "And will not God vindicate his elect, who cry to him day and night? Will he delay long over them? I tell you, he will vindicate them speedily. Nevertheless, when the Son of man comes, will he find faith on earth?" (Luke 18:7–8).

In the face of Israel's common plight, the rift between the synagogue and the church was probably unavoidable. Christian confidence in the vindication of the crucified messiah-prophet Jesus and readiness to apply all the scriptures to him would accommodate little compromise with contrary or even alternative views. The gentile question threatened to divide the Christian community from within and left it open to charges of apostasy from the faith and practice of Israel. Christian eschatological hopes and perspectives on the present as a new day, awaiting only the full disclosure of the divine apocalypse, raised a challenge both through a disinctively messianic message and through innovations with the traditions. Then, as the Jewish nation, cultus, and people faced the grave peril of destruction, the common trust in God's promises to faithful Israel demanded severe measures for cleansing Israel's infidelity.[5]

In spite of its comparatively congenial stance toward the Pharisees and its consistent presentation of the faithful observance of the law by Jewish Christians, Luke's narrative does not obscure caustic denominational polemics. His is not so much a theology of history in which the past justifies present good fortunes or an apocalyptic schema in which the hope of future vindication preoccupies the dreams of the hopeless, although both of those categories are helpful for describing crucial aspects of his work. But the evangelist has reaffirmed the prophetic vision of God's continuing involvement within history in judgment and salvation through the anointed prophet and exalted Lord.

The grand sweep and proportions of Luke's narrative do evoke its larger cultural setting, especially since the courage and confidence with which Luke assured his readers were then in short supply among the victors as well as the vanquished. The glorious promise of the golden age of Augustus, with the savior-benefactors manifesting the generosity of divine providence for all humanity, was now often perceived as empty, if not false, prophecy. Abuses of power, followed by assassinations and coups within the imperial ranks, disruptions of social structures, and ensuing economic chaos threatened to produce a failure of nerve in which many duty-bound Romans would languish. Therefore, Luke's mission theology as a messianist scriptural commentary and critique of such imperial rhetoric and ideology merits considerably more attention.[6] Clearly, Luke does intend to equip the church to come to terms with that vast political, philosophical, and religious discussion by means of an audacious vision of God's providence through the exalted messiah and Lord, Jesus.

But the fiber and fabric of that bold assurance can only be measured by the standard of its *interpretation of the times* within the experience of Israel. No easy spiritualizing or apocalyptic escapes are offered to avoid confronting the mysteries of the rejection of the prophet-messiah, his crucifixion at the hands of Israel and the Gentiles, and the destruction of the holy city and temple. Nor is the Christian mission founded on its rejection by Israel.

Faith is found *within* Israel, and the mission to the Gentiles proceeds out of that faith. Even the reproof of Israel's obduracy, which the premature inclusion of the Gentiles intensifies, still affirms God's faithfulness in accord with all the scriptural warnings and promises to Israel and the Gentiles. Finally, the weal and woe of the theocentric prophetic vision of Israel's calling, election, and vocation in the world are also marshaled by Luke to offer a pastoral assurance to a community in troubled times: "Fear not, little flock, for it is your Father's good pleasure to give you the kingdom" (Luke 12:32).

Notes

Chapter 1—The Narrative Gospel

1. Philo, *Ad Gaium*. Josephus *Antiquities* 18.261–309, *War* 2.184–87, 192–203. See Victor Tcherikover, *Corpus Papyrorum Judaicarum*, vol. 1 (Cambridge, Mass.: Harvard University Press, 1957). E. Mary Small-wood, *The Jews under Roman Rule*, Studies in Judaism in Late Antiquity 20 (Leiden: E. J. Brill, 1976), pp. 212–88.

2. Tacitus *Histories* 5.9. Josephus *Antiquities* 20.256–57, *War* 2.279.

3. Jacob Neusner, *A Life of Yohanan ben Zakkai*, Studia Post-Biblica 6 (Leiden: E. J. Brill, 1970), pp. 177–78.

4. Josephus *War* 5.362–419.

5. Ibid., 6.281–87.

6. See E. R. Dodds, *Christian and Pagan in an Age of Anxiety* (Cambridge: Cambridge University Press, 1965). Max Pohlenz, *Freedom in Greek Life and Thought* (Dordrecht: D. Reidel, 1966).

7. The debate concerning the place rhetorical eloquence and dramatic effect had in the writing of history often produced caustic criticism among the historians of the era. See Polybius 2.56 where drama is contrasted with history, a comment that could well be a critique of most contemporary historiography. See also Cicero's *Brutus* 262 and, in contrast, Lucian *How to Write History* 53–55.

8. Tacitus *Histories* 1.3.

9. *Moralia* 549B, 551E.

10. An immense literature on comparative midrash and ancient methods of exegesis has emerged in recent years, which sheds light on the hermeneutical dimensions of Jewish traditions and groups in the Greco-Roman era. For discussion of the apologetic-propagandistic aspects of

such exegesis, see Dieter Georgi, *Die Gegner des Paulus im 2 Korintherbrief,* WMANT 11 (Neukirchen-Vluyn: Neukirchener Verlag, 1964), pp. 168–82. Victor Tcherikover, "Jewish Apologetic Literature Reconsidered," *Eos* 48,3 (1956), pp. 169–93. David L. Tiede, "Religious Propaganda and the Gospel Literature of the Early Christian Mission," due to appear in *Aufstieg und Niedergang der römischen Welt,* vol. 16 (Berlin: de Gruyter, –).

11. The term "biblical theology" is thus anachronistic, at least before the establishment of a fixed text in the late first or early second century and probably until the time of the great codices of the Greek church. The difference between possessing sacred scriptures, perhaps collected as scrolls in a genizah or as letters and books, and having a "bible" bound in one codex dramatically affects the understanding of norm or canon that is operative.

12. See Paul D. Hanson, *The Dawn of Apocalyptic* (Philadelphia: Fortress Press, 1975).

13. On the theme of judgment for refusing to listen to the prophet, see also Jer. 26:20–24; 35:14–15; 2 Chron. 12:5–8; 21:12–15; 25:7–9, 15–17; 26:16(!). For the broad development of the theme in Prov. 1: 24–33 of judgment for refusal to listen to God's wisdom, see Burton Mack, "Wisdom Myth and Mythology," *Interpretation* 29 (1970):46–60.

14. See Henry J. Cadbury, "The Greek and Jewish Traditions of Writing History," *The Beginnings of Christianity,* ed. F. J. Foakes Jackson and Kirsopp Lake, vol. 2 (London: Macmillan, 1922), pp. 7–29. See also Cadbury's discussion of Josephus's adaptation of 1 Maccabees in *Antiquities* 12.240–13.211 in *The Making of Luke–Acts* (London: SPCK, 1961, first published 1927), pp. 169–83. The histories of *Jubilees, The Testament of Moses,* and pseudo-Philo's *Biblical Antiquities* should also be compared to document the prevalence of this archaizing "scriptural" historiography. See chapter 2, note 66.

15. "The Gospels and the Canonical Process: A Response to Lou H. Silberman," *The Relationship among the Gospels* (San Antonio: Trinity University Press, 1978), p. 235. See also the discussion of Luke's peculiar intention to be "biblical," that is, imitative of the authoritative scriptural tradition as well as paraphrastic or midrashic by Joseph A. Fitzmyer, "Judaic Studies and the Gospels," ibid., p. 253.

16. Josephus *War* 5.399–412.

17. Ibid., 6.333–46.

18. See 4 Ezra 4–8, 2 Baruch 2–4, Alden Lloyd Thompson, *Responsibility for Evil in the Theodicy of IV Ezra,* SBLDS 29 (Missoula: Scholars Press, 1977).

19. See note 10 above and David Daube, "Rabbinic Methods of Interpretation and Hellenistic Rhetoric," *Hebrew Union College Annual*

22 (1949):239–64. Henry A. Fischel, ed., *Essays in Greco-Roman and Related Talmudic Literature* (New York: KTAV, 1977).

20. See David S. Winston, "Freedom and Determinism in Greek Philosophy and Jewish Hellenistic Wisdom," *Studia Philonica* 2 (1973): 40–52.

21. See Martin Hengel, *Judaism and Hellenism,* vol. 1 (Philadelphia: Fortress Press, 1974), pp. 1–5.

22. Jacob Jervell, "The Divided People of God," *Luke and the People of God* (Minneapolis: Augsburg Publishing House, 1972). S. Stowers, "The Synagogue in the Theology of Acts," *Restoration Quarterly* 17 (1974):129–43. On the centrality of the synagogue to Jewish identity in this era, see Jonathan Z. Smith, "Fences and Neighbors: The Contours of Early Judaism." Society of Biblical Literature Centennial Lecture, November 19, 1978.

23. The term "Jew" generally belongs to the vocabulary of the Greek or Roman "outsiders" while the term "Israel" is the preferred self-designation. See, for example, the opening chapters of 1 Maccabees, but note that the term "Jew" can also be a self-designation as in 1 Macc. 8:20 and 12:6. See Walter Gutbrod, *"Israel, Ioudaios, Hebraios* in Greek Hellenistic Literature," *Theological Dictionary of the New Testament,* ed. Gerhard Kittel, trans. G. W. Bromiley, vol. 3 (Grand Rapids: Eerdmans, 1966), pp. 369–91. The use of the term "Jew" as a synonym for those who oppose Christ as preached by the apostles finds resonance in the Gospel of John, but is far from uniform in Acts. See Richard F. Zehnle, *Peter's Pentecost Discourse,* SBLMS 15 (Nashville: Abington Press, 1971), p. 65.

24. Samuel Sandmel, *Philo's Place in Judaism: A Study of Conceptions of Abraham in Jewish Literature, Augmented* (New York: KTAV, 1971), p. 211.

25. See especially Luke 2:1–2; 3:1–2,23–38; 16:16; 23:1–39; 24:27, 44; Acts 3:13; 7:1–50; 11:28; 13:16–41.

26. See Thucydides (II,2,1) and his hellenistic imitators such as Dionysius of Halicarnassus (*Roman Antiquities* 9.61), Josephus (*War* 2.284, *Antiquities* 20.257). Cadbury, *The Making of Luke–Acts,* pp. 204–9.

27. On the concept of the hellenistic benefactor, see Frederick W. Danker, *Luke,* Proclamation Commentaries (Philadelphia: Fortress Press, 1976). On the literary genre of biography, especially as related to its use to identify authoritative traditions in philosophical schools, see Charles H. Talbert, *Literary Patterns, Theological Themes and the Genre of Luke–Acts,* SBLMS 20 (Missoula: Scholars Press, 1974), and *What Is a Gospel?* (Philadelphia: Fortress Press, 1977). On the prophetic content of Luke's treatment of the succession of Jesus and the apostles,

see Luke T. Johnson, *The Literary Function of Possessions in Luke–Acts,* SBLDS 40 (Missoula: Scholars Press, 1976).

28. Ostensibly objective scholarship is never far from the theological and historical battlefield, as recent studies in Luke–Acts reveal dramatically. The issue is joined frontally from a declared position with good bibliographic research by W. G. Kümmel in "Current Theological Accusations Against Luke," *Andover Newton Quarterly* 16 (1975):131–45.

29. The case was made most forcefully in the 1950 essay by Philip Vielhauer, now published in English, "On the 'Paulinism' of Acts," *Studies in Luke–Acts,* ed. Leander E. Keck and J. Louis Martyn (Philadelphia: Fortress Press, 1980), pp. 33–50.

30. See Charles H. Talbert, "Shifting Sands: The Recent Study of the Gospel of Luke," *Interpretation* 30 (1976):381–95

31. See note 28 above, but particular attention must be given to Ernst Käsemann's 1953 essay on "The Problem of the 'Historical Jesus,'" *Essays on New Testament Themes,* Studies in Biblical Theology 41 (London: SCM Press, 1964), pp. 15–47. Käsemann hails Conzelmann's work for demonstrating how in Luke "primitive Christian eschatology is replaced by salvation history, which is characterized by an historically verifiable continuity and by a process of ever-extending development" (p. 28) and argues that "revelation ceases to be God's revelation once it has been brought within a causal nexus" (p. 31). Such a caricature of Luke's "redaction" and such historical "docetism" have had a profound effect on subsequent interpretations of Luke–Acts.

32. See especially Paul S. Minear, "Luke's Use of the Birth Stories," *Studies in Luke–Acts,* pp. 111–30.

33. See Paul Schubert, "The Structure and Significance of Luke 24," *Neutestamentliche Studien für Rudolf Bultmann,* ZNW Beiheft 21 (Berlin: Töpelmann, 1954), pp. 165–86.

34. Norman Petersen, *Literary Criticism for New Testament Critics,* Guides to Biblical Scholarship (Philadelphia: Fortress Press, 1978), p. 83.

35. See Robert Wilken, *The Myth of Christian Beginnings* (Garden City, N.Y.: Doubleday, 1971).

36. See Paul S. Minear, "Dear Theo: The Kerygmatic Intention and Claim of the Book of Acts," *Interpretation* 27 (1973):131–50. Frieder Schütz, *Der leidende Christus: Die angefochtene Gemeinde und das Christuskerygma der lukanischen Schriften* (Stuttgart: Kohlhammer, 1968).

37. Perhaps such eschatological-theological conflicts are fundamental to the purpose of the book. On Luke as contending with apocalypticism, see E. Earle Ellis, *Eschatology in Luke,* Facet Books; Biblical Series 30

(Philadelphia: Fortress Press, 1972). Frederick W. Danker, *Jesus and the New Age* (St. Louis: Clayton Publishing House, 1972). On the possibility that Luke is contending with an extreme spiritualized or gnosticizing theology, see Charles H. Talbert, *Luke and the Gnostics* (Nashville: Abingdon Press, 1966).

38. This has been shown most effectively in the case of traditions about possessions and money by Johnson, *The Literary Function of Possessions in Luke–Acts.*

39. Carl E. Braaten, *History and Hermeneutics,* New Directions in Theology Today, vol. 2 (Philadelphia: Westminster Press, 1966), p. 52.

Chapter 2—No Prophet Is Acceptable in His Own Country

1. See especially Hans Conzelmann, *The Theology of St. Luke,* trans. Geoffrey Buswell (New York: Harper & Row, 1960).

2. Hugh Anderson, "Broadening Horizons: The Rejection at Nazareth Pericope of Luke 4:16–30 in the Light of Recent Critical Trends," *Interpretation* 18 (1964):272.

3. Paul S. Minear, "Luke's Use of the Birth Stories," *Studies in Luke–Acts,* ed. Leander E. Keck and J. Louis Martyn (Philadelphia: Fortress Press, 1980), p. 125. See also the efforts to remedy Conzelmann's neglect of Luke 1–2 while maintaining his "salvation history" approach: H. H. Oliver, "The Lucan Birth Stories and the Purpose of Luke–Acts," *New Testament Studies* 10 (1964):202–6; and W. B. Tatum, "The Epoch of Israel: Luke i–ii and the Theological Plan of Luke–Acts," *New Testament Studies* 13 (1967):184–95.

4. Note especially the close parallels with Mary's song of thanksgiving (Luke 1:46–55) and Hannah's song (1 Sam. 2:1–10). For a comprehensive discussion of these passages, see Raymond E. Brown, *The Birth of the Messiah* (Garden City, N.Y.: Doubleday, 1977).

5. See below in chapter 3 where the scriptural usage of "because" (*anth hōn*) in contexts of judgment is discussed.

6. Even John's harsh words of indictment in Luke 3:7–9 are not directed toward an opposition within the crowds (see the Pharisees and Sadducees in Matt. 3:7–10). In Luke, the multitudes who are castigated appear to be identical with the repentant (3:7,10). Nor is there any royal plot on the life of the child Jesus in Luke.

7. See Heinz Schürmann, *Das Lukasevangelium* (Freiburg: Herder, 1969), p. 126. The intricate use and alteration of the text of Isaiah in this passage also deserves more thorough explication, especially since the term "people" is played upon, first to include the Gentiles and then limited to Israel (2:31–32). See Nils A. Dahl, "A People for His Name

(Acts 15:4)," *New Testament Studies* 4 (1957):319–27, and below, chapter 4, note 23.

8. E.g., the phrase "and a sword will pierce through your own soul also" (2:35a) remains elusive in spite of considerable scribal activity and historical speculation.

9. See Robert J. Karris, *What Are They Saying about the Gospel of Luke and Acts?: A Theology of the Faithful God* (New York: Paulist Press, 1979).

10. See the frequent use of the terms *dei, mellein, exestin,* and *anagkē.*

11. See also the magi and the star in Matthew 2.

12. Note especially Walter Grundmann, *"dei," Theological Dictionary of the New Testament,* vol. 2, pp. 21–25. E. Fascher, "Theologische Beobachtungen zu *dei* im alten Testament," *Zeitschrift für die Neutestamentliche Wissenschaft* 45 (1954):244–52. *Neutestamentliche Studien für Rudolf Bultmann,* ZNW Beiheft 21 (Berlin: Töpelmann, 1954), pp. 228–54.

13. See literature in chapter 1, notes 6, 13, and 20, plus David S. Winston, "Freedom and Determinism in Philo of Alexandria," *Studia Philonica* 3(1974–1975):47–70.

14. See, for example, the Stoic and middle Platonic doctrines of the freedom of the *sophos* as presented by Philo. David L. Tiede, *The Charismatic Figure as Miracle Worker,* SBLDS 1 (Missoula: Scholars Press, 1972), pp. 101–37.

15. Josephus *Antiquities* 13.172–73, trans. Ralph Marcus, Loeb ed. (Cambridge, Mass.: Harvard University Press, 1943). See also *Antiquities* 18.12–25, Josephus *War* 2.119–66. *Pirke Aboth* 3.19, "Everything is foreseen, yet freedom of choice is given."

16. See Alden Lloyd Thompson, *Responsibility for Evil in the Theodicy of IV Ezra,* SBLDS 29 (Missoula: Scholars Press, 1977). James L. Crenshaw, "The Problem of Theodicy in Sirach: On Human Bondage," *Journal of Biblical Literature* 94 (1975):47–64.

17. Or compare the Qumran *War Scroll* 11:7 as a scriptural commentary on Num. 24:17–19, "By the hand of Thine anointed, who discerned Thy testimonies, Thou hast revealed to us the times of the battles of Thy hands that Thou mayest glorify Thyself in our enemies by leveling the hordes of Satan," trans. G. Vermes, *The Dead Sea Scrolls in English* (Middlesex: Penguin, 1962, p. 138.

18. The question is worthy of considerably more attention than will be possible in this study. Close comparison of contemporary "midrashic" or interpretive usages of the authoritative Jewish texts promises to give a more precise reading of Luke's usage. Even now as such research is being pursued, certain recognizable traditions of interpretation such as that of Qumran, Philo, and the targums can provide points of contrast.

See Merrill P. Miller, "Targum, Midrash and the Use of the Old Testament in the New Testament," *Journal of the Study of Judaism* 2 (1971): 29–82. Renée Bloch, "Midrash," trans. Mary Howard Callaway, *Approaches to Ancient Judaism: Theory and Practice,* Brown Judaic Studies 1 (Missoula: Scholars Press, 1978), pp. 29–50.

19. See especially accounts of the call of the prophet in Isaiah 6 and 1 Kings 22:21.

20. See Acts 3:17–28; Deut. 18:15–19; plus Lev. 23:29. The midrashic "enrichment" of the text from Deuteronomy is discussed below.

21. See Henry J. Cadbury, *The Making of Luke–Acts* (London: SPCK, 1961, first published 1927), p. 316. I. H. Marshall, *Luke: Historian and Theologian* (Grand Rapids: Zondervan, 1970), pp. 37–44.

22. Abraham J. Heschel, *The Prophets* (New York: Harper & Row, 1962), pp. 190–91.

23. Ibid., p. 74. See also Gerhard von Rad, *Old Testament Theology,* vol. 2 (New York: Harper & Row, 1965), pp. 422–29. For a contrary view of Luke's concept of necessity, prophecy, and history, see Siegfried Schulz, "Gottes Vorsehung bei Lukas," *Zeitschrift für die Neutestamentliche Wissenschaft* 54 (1963):104–216.

24. Klaus Baltzer, "The Meaning of the Temple in the Lukan Writings," *Harvard Theological Review* 58 (1965):263–77.

25. Conzelmann, *The Theology of St. Luke,* p. 28.

26. See Charles H. Talbert, *Literary Patterns, Theological Themes and the Genre of Luke–Acts,* SBLMS 20 (Missoula: Scholars Press, 1975).

27. This is a modified version of the analysis of Nils Wilhelm Lund, *Chaismus in the New Testament* (Chapel Hill: University of North Carolina Press, 1942), p. 236. See also Donald R. Miesner, "The Circumferential Speeches of Luke–Acts: Patterns and Purpose," *Seminar Papers* 14, vol. 2, Society of Biblical Literature, ed. Paul J. Achtemeier (Missoula: Scholars Press, 1978), pp. 223–37.

28. See Larrimore C. Crockett, "The Old Testament in the Gospel of Luke" (Ph.D. diss.: Brown University, 1966), pp. 63, 279–80. Note the manuscript variation concerning the reading.

29. See also Luke 22:56 (inspection/accusation) and Acts 3:12 (gaze/adoration).

30. See J. Bajard, "La Structure de la Pericope de Nazareth en Lc IV 16–30," *Ephemerides theologicae Louvanienses* 45 (1969):165–71.

31. Compare the juridical language in diverse prophetic accounts, but especially in the "trial speeches" of 2 Isaiah where both the nations and the prophet's own people are placed in the docket: 41:1–5,21–29; 43:8–15; 44:6–8; 45:20–25. See also the specific disputes with Israel where God appears to respond to laments of not having seen or heard the peo-

ple's plight by charging them with deafness and blindness, 40:12–31 (especially v. 27) and 42:18–25. See Claus Westermann, *Isaiah 40–66* (Philadelphia: Westminster Press, 1969), pp. 15, 109.

32. In addition to the passages mentioned in note 31 above, see Job 38:1–42:6. Of course, the technique of turning accusations into indictments is not at all limited to the Jewish prophetic scriptures, but the explicit references to Isaiah make those precedents particularly attractive.

33. See I. H. Marshall, *The Gospel of Luke* (Grand Rapids: Eerdmans, 1978), p. 190, "The shadow of rejection hangs over the ministry of Jesus from the outset."

34. As might be expected, the problems in manuscript transmission become very complex in these references to Joseph.

35. The speeches are, in general, to be regarded as Lucan compositions. Whatever sources lie behind them, as they stand in their contexts, they have been brought to the service of the purposes of the narrative. See Henry J. Cadbury, "The Speeches in Acts," *Beginnings of Christianity,* vol. 5 (1933):402–27. Martin Dibelius, "The Speeches in Acts and Ancient Historiography," *Studies in the Acts of the Apostles* (London: SCM Press, 1956), pp. 138–85. Ulrich Wilckens, *Die Missionsreden der Apostelgeschichte,* WMANT 5 (Neukirchen: Neukirchener Verlag, 1963).

36. The textual problems in Acts 13:27 serve to highlight the close juxtaposition of Jesus (*touton*) and the utterances of the prophets as subjects of the ignorance or misunderstanding of the people and their rulers.

37. See von Rad, *Old Testament Theology,* p. 261, note 42, for an exposition of the deuteronomic preoccupation with Moses as "servant of God" and its connection with the servant of God in deutero-Isaiah. See also p. 276 concerning the vicarious suffering of the prophetic servant on behalf of Israel. On the development of this tradition up to the New Testament era, see Odil Hannes Steck, *Israel und das gewaltsame Geschick der Propheten,* WMANT 23 (Neukirchen: Neukirchener Verlag, 1967).

38. See also Howard M. Teeple, *The Mosaic Eschatological Prophet,* SBLMS 10 (Philadelphia: Society of Biblical Literature, 1957). Joachim Jeremias, "Mousēs," *Theological Dictionary of the New Testament,* vol. 4, pp. 848–73.

39. It is at least worth noting that even within the book of Joshua, Joshua's parting of the Jordan was viewed as God's verification of him as Moses' successor: "This day I will begin to exalt you in the sight of all Israel, that they may know that, as I was with Moses, so I will be with you" (Josh. 3:7). Josephus's account of the appointment of Joshua/ Jesus as Moses' successor also expands on the text of Numbers 27 to

specify that Joshua was to be the *diadochos* both in "prophecies" and as "general." Joshua/Jesus is thus already identified as the prophet like Moses (*Antiquities* 4.165). Furthermore, Josephus's accounts of diverse "prophets" who sought to stir up a new "exodus" or otherwise liberate Israel from bondage suggests that several were playing the role of a Joshua as successors to Moses. See Tiede, *The Charismatic Figure as Miracle Worker*, pp. 101–240, especially pp. 197–206. Frederick W. Danker, *Luke*, Proclamation Commentaries (Philadelphia: Fortress Press, 1976), p. 8.

40. See "The Martyrdom of Isaiah," in R. H. Charles, *Pseudepigrapha of the Old Testament* (Oxford: Clarendon Press, 1913), pp. 155–62, and Josephus's *Antiquities* 10.38 as expansions of 2 Kings 21:16. See also Steck, cited in note 37 above.

41. See Luke 6:23 (Matt. 5:12); 7:26, 33–35; 9:8–9, 19–22; 11:47–51 (Matt. 23); 13:33–35 (Matt. 23:37–39); 16:29–30; Acts 7:35–53.

42. See chapter 4, The Definite Plan and Foreknowledge of God.

43. See James A. Sanders, "From Isaiah 61 to Luke 4," *Christianity, Judaism and Other Greco-Roman Cults*, Studies in Honor of Morton Smith, ed. J. Neusner, vol. 1 (Leiden: E. J. Brill, 1975), pp. 80–82.

44. von Rad, *Old Testament Theology*, pp. 238–62.

45. Luke 3:22; Acts 2:4,17; 4:27; 10:36–38. See also Num. 11:26–30.

46. See Ps. 89:3 (88:4) where "my chosen" is singular in Hebrew, referring to David, but plural in the Septuagint, extending to Israel and v. 20 (21). See also Psalm 132 (131), where the election of Zion rests on the oath to David the anointed servant and 2 Samuel 7, 1 Kings 11: 13,32; 2 Kings 19:34; 20:6; 2 Chron. 6:41–42; and the allusions to Psalms 2 and 16 and Isaiah 55 in Acts 13:33–37.

47. See Hebrew *ebed* translated in crucial passages concerning Moses' prophecy as *therapōn* in Num. 12:7–8 (compare Exod. 14:31) and as *oiketēs* in Deut. 34:5 and frequently as *pais* in Joshua; 2 Chron. 24:9. In Neh. 1:7–8 and Dan. 9:11, the reference to Moses as *pais* appears in the context of prayers confessing Israel's unfaithfulness, and this same concern is developed in references to Moses and all the prophets as *paides* of God in Bar. 1:20; 2:20,24,28 (note especially the usage of Deuteronomy 28 and Jeremiah 32 in Bar. 1:1–3:8). In chapter 3 below, the continuing force of Moses' parting blessings and curses (Deuteronomy 32) in Josephus and 2 Baruch's interpretation of the Roman destruction will be discussed.

48. Note the vocabulary of "leading out" used of Moses in Acts 7:36,40 and God in Acts 13:17. Note also the volatility of this "exodus" language in Acts 21:38 (see Tiede, *The Charismatic Figure as Miracle Worker*, pp. 178–206).

49. See J. Blinzer, "The Jewish Punishment of Stoning in the New

141

Testament Period," *The Trial of Jesus,* Cambridge Studies in Honour of C. F. D. Moule, ed. E. Bammel; Studies in Biblical Theology, second series, 13 (London: SCM Press, 1970) pp. 147–61. Note also that when Jesus is taunted to "prophesy" during his arrest, Luke specifically accuses his accusers of "blasphemy" (Luke 22:65).

50. "From Isaiah 61 to Luke 4," p. 99.

51. Ibid., p. 101.

52. Crockett, "The Old Testament in the Gospel of Luke," and "Luke 4:25–27 and Jewish-Gentile Relations in Luke–Acts," *Journal of Biblical Literature* 88 (1969), see pp. 179–81.

53. Crockett, "The Old Testament in the Gospel of Luke," p. 282.

54. See also James A. Sanders, "The Ethic of Election in Luke's Great Banquet Parable," *Essays in Old Testament Ethics,* J. Philip Hyatt, in Memoriam, ed. James L. Crenshaw and John T. Willis (New York: KTAV, 1974), pp. 245–71.

55. Crockett, "The Old Testament in the Gospel of Luke," p. 275. See especially Sirach 48.

56. Heschel, *The Prophets,* p. 176.

57. See Jacob Jervell, "The Lost Sheep of the House of Israel," *Luke and the People of God* (Minneapolis: Augsburg Publishing House, 1972), pp. 113–32.

58. See the correspondences between this pronouncement and 9:56a in alternative textual readings: "For the son of man came not to destroy men's lives but to save them."

59. So, Eric Franklin, *Christ the Lord* (Philadelphia: Westminster Press, 1975), p. 79: "The ascension binds the whole of God's saving history into a single action and gives meaning to it in its totality. This is the fulfillment of God's promises."

60. Jesus' purposeful journey has, of course, been kept before the reader since before his appearance in Nazareth (e.g., 4:14–15, 30,43, and again in 8:1–3), and it is repeatedly mentioned in subsequent passages (9:57; 10:1,38; 11:53; 13:22,33; 17:11; 18:31,35; 19:1).

61. See especially the popular *periplous* genre as discussed by Cadbury, *The Making of Luke–Acts,* pp. 60, 144. Vernon K. Robbins, "By Land and by Sea: The We-Passages and Ancient Sea Voyages," *Perspectives on Luke–Acts,* Perspectives in Religious Studies, Special Studies Series 5, ed. Charles H. Talbert (Danville, Va.: Association of Baptist Professors of Religion, 1978), pp. 215–42.

62. On the persistent freighting of the term "to go" (*poreuesthai*), see David Gill, "Observations on the Lukan Travel Narrative and Some Related Passages," *Harvard Theological Review* 63 (1970):199–221. See also William C. Robinson, "The Way of the Lord" (Doctoral diss.: Basel, 1962).

63. Comparing Luke's separation of the passion predictions (9:22;

2:43b–45; 18:31–34) with Mark's (8:31–33; 9:30–32; 10:32–34) displays the contrast in the timing of the respective narratives. See David L. Tiede, "The Gospel for the Duration," *The Lutheran Quarterly* 26 (1974):225–31.

64. C. F. Evans, "The Central Section of St. Luke's Gospel," *Studies in the Gospels*, Essays in Memory of R. H. Lightfoot, ed. D. E. Nineham (Oxford: Blackwell, 1955), pp. 37–53. See p. 40.

65. See David L. Tiede, "The Figure of Moses," in *The Testament of Moses*, Society of Biblical Literature, Septuagint and Cognate Studies 4 (Missoula: Scholars Press, 1973), pp. 86–92.

66. Daniel J. Harrington, "Interpreting Israel's History: *The Testament of Moses* as a Rewriting of Deut. 31–34," *Studies in the Testament of Moses*, pp. 59–68. See also En. 103:9–12 and the Testament of Moses on Deuteronomy 28 as described by George W. E. Nickelsburg, Jr., *Resurrection, Immortality, and Eternal Life in Intertestamental Judaism*, Harvard Theological Studies 26 (Cambridge, Mass.: Harvard University Press, 1972), pp. 29, 44, 119.

67. The Septuagint adds that the nations shall be utterly destroyed, Deut. 33:19. See Luke 2:29–32; Acts 2:39; 3:25; 13:47.

68. Note also that the Elijah story in Luke 4 stresses the "cleansing" of a Gentile. But Luke also presents the cleansing of Jewish and Samaritan lepers (5:12–16; 17:14–17), and rehearses one of his few polemics against the Pharisees for being too concerned with external cleansing (11:37–54).

69. The clustering of vocabulary similar to Luke 9:51–57 in Deuteronomy 1 is noteworthy. See (*eis-*) (*pro-*) *poreuesthai* in 1:7,8,19,22, 30,32,33, *hodos* in 1:2,19,22,31,33,40, *prosōpon* in 1:21,30.

70. Note the Masoretic Text of Ezek. 21:2, "Son of man set your face toward Jerusalem and preach against the sanctuaries; prophesy against the land of Israel." In a Claremont graduate seminar paper, Craig A. Evans has explored the close correlation of this vocabulary with that of Luke 9:51–54 against the background of ancient traditions of official emissaries.

Chapter 3—Weeping for Jerusalem

1. See Victor Tcherikover, *Hellenistic Civilization and the Jews* (Philadelphia: Jewish Publication Society, 1959).

2. See especially the Qumran commentary on Habakkuk XII and Josephus *Antiquities* 13.288–98,398–418.

3. Josephus *War* 7.300–9 and Jer. 7:34 et passim. Josephus does not call him a "prophet," but allows that he was driven by a "supernatural impulse" (See translation by H. St. J. Thackeray, Loeb ed., 1928.) See

David L. Tiede, *The Charismatic Figure as Miracle Worker*, SBLDS 1 (Missoula: Scholars Press, 1972), pp. 101–240, especially 197–206.

4. The bathos of the "Homily on the Passion" by Melito of Sardis is a good example of such feigned sorrow at the expense of "lawless Israel" in order to justify the subsequent suffering of the Jews: "[all these afflictions] from him, O Israel, you have brought upon yourself," p. 13, 1 (79). See also Origen, *Contra Celsum* 1.47; 2.8,14 (citing Luke 21:20); 4.22,32,73; 8.42,69 where the direct link is made between the death of Jesus and the destruction of Jerusalem in terms of indictment.

5. C. H. Dodd, "The Fall of Jerusalem and the 'Abomination of Desolation,' " *Journal of Roman Studies* 37 (1947):47–54: reprinted in *More New Testament Studies* (Manchester: Manchester University Press, 1968), pp. 69–83, see p. 79. John A. T. Robinson, *Redating the New Testament* (Philadelphia: Westminster Press, 1976), refers to Dodd's article as support for a possible pre-70 date for Luke–Acts, correctly noting that it has removed a crucial argument for the dating of the Gospel but failing to acknowledge that Dodd did not, therefore, regard Luke as a prewar composition.

6. Lloyd Gaston, *No Stone on Another: Studies in the Significance of the Fall of Jerusalem in the Synoptic Gospels*, Supplements to *Novum Testamentum* 23 (Leiden: E. J. Brill, 1970), pp. 364, 368–69.

7. Ibid., pp. 255–56, depending heavily upon H. Sahlin, *Der Messias und das Gottesvolk: Studien zur Protolukanische Theologie* (Uppsala, 1945).

8. See S. G. Wilson, *The Gentiles and the Gentile Mission in Luke–Acts*, SNTS Monograph Series 23 (New York: Cambridge University Press, 1973), p. 255. On Luke as a pastoral theologian, see also Paul S. Minear, "Dear Theo: The Kerygmatic Intention and Claim of the Book of Acts," *Interpretation* 27 (1973):131–50; E. A. La Verdiere and William G. Thompson, "New Testament Communities in Transition: A Study of Matthew and Luke," *Theological Studies* 37 (1976):567–97; Robert J. Karris, "Missionary Communities: A New Paradigm for the Study of Luke–Acts," *Catholic Biblical Quarterly* 41 (1979):80–97.

9. See Charles H. Talbert, *Literary Patterns, Theological Themes, and the Genre of Luke–Acts*, SBLMS 20 (Missoula: Scholars Press, 1974), pp. 51–56. Note that Talbert (following Goulder) marks 18:30 as the terminus of the chiasm so that 18:31 would be resumptive.

10. The text is very questionable at this point, but even if the precise indicative references to time "when" are suspect, the usage of the phrase in Luke 19:38 supports such a translation.

11. See especially Paul Schubert, "The Structure and Significance of Luke 24," *Neutestamentliche Studien für Rudolf Bultmann*, ZNW Beiheft 21 (Berlin: Töpelmann, 1954).

12. See David L. Dungan, "The New Testament Canon in Recent Study," *Interpretation* 29 (1975):339–51.

13. See C. H. Dodd, *According to the Scriptures* (Digswell Place: James Nisbet, 1952), p. 136, where these alternatives are offered as a helpful corrective to an earlier neglect of the scriptural bases of New Testament theology.

14. C. F. Evans, "The Central Section of St. Luke's Gospel," *Studies in the Gospels*, Essays in Memory of R. H. Lightfoot, ed. D. E. Nineham (Oxford: Blackwell, 1955), pp. 37–53. James A. Sanders, "The Ethic of Election in Luke's Great Banquet Parable," *Essays in Old Testament Ethics*, J. Philip Hyatt, in memoriam, ed. James L. Crenshaw (New York: KTAV, 1974), pp. 245–71.

15. A wooden "Heilsgeschichte" reading of the "Travel Narrative" falls easy prey to such reductionism, as displayed most blatantly in Helmuth L. Egelkraut, *Jesus' Mission to Jerusalem: A Redaction-Critical Study of the Travel Narrative in the Gospel of Luke*, Luke 9:51–19:48, Europäische Hochschulschriften 23 (Frankfurt: Peter Lang, 1976). See especially p. 218: "Once Jerusalem falls there is no longer an Israel, but a host of Jews who gather in their synagogues but lack any visible center." And p. 229: "since this persistent effort of the apostles is persistently answered with hostility, it can only mean two things: First, the Jews are a totally hopeless case. Second: Luke wants to show in historical categories how Israel, once it was rejected (Travel Narrative), systematically excluded itself from salvation and is thus no longer the legitimate guardian of God's revelation."

16. On the persistence of the motif of the suffering prophet and of the Deuteronomic vocabulary, see Odil Hannes Steck, *Israel und das gewaltsame Geschick der Propheten*, WMANT 23 (Neukirchen: Neukirchener Verlag, 1967), and Moshe Weinfeld, *Deuteronomy and the Deuteronomic School* (Oxford: Clarendon Press, 1972). See Jer. 26:20–23; 2 Chron. 24:20–22; 1 Kings 19:10; and Josephus's expansion of the story of the evils of Manasseh to include the killing of the prophets, *Antiquities* 10.38.

17. Klaus Baltzer, "The Meaning of the Temple in the Lukan Writings," *Harvard Theological Review* 58 (1965):273.

18. To be sure, Luke does take into account problems associated with the delay of the Lord's return, e.g., 12:38,45; 13:8; 18:7; 20:9; 21:9. See William C. Robinson, Jr., "Luke, Gospel of," *The Interpreter's Dictionary of the Bible*, Supplementary Vol. (Nashville: Abingdon Press, 1976), pp. 558–60. But this pastoral problem is not the occasion for such a comprehensive "apology" as it might appear when judged from the standard of Mark. Indeed, the "delay" is viewed by Luke as divine intervention, separating Jesus' arrival in Jerusalem as a "visitation" from

the return in judgment. "God intervenes not to shorten the days, but to give the unrepentant still another chance." Henry J. Cadbury, *The Making of Luke–Acts* (London: SPCK, 1961, first published 1927), p. 296.

19. The use of the future tense in the apodosis is preferred over the less well attested future perfect. Furthermore, it corresponds to Luke's use of the future tense in Jesus' rejoinder to the *ad hominem* question in Nazareth: "And no doubt you will quote the old bromide at me, 'Physician heal yourself' . . ." (4:23–24, author's translation).

20. Of these references only the allusion to Psalm 118 is found in Luke's probable source, Mark, and the parallel to Luke 20:18 in Matt. 21:24 is textually suspect of harmonization.

21. William Manson, *The Gospel of Luke*, The Moffat New Testament Commentary (London: Hodder and Stoughton, 1930), pp. 216–17. Adolph Schlatter, *Das Evangelium des Lukas* (Stuttgart, 1960), has, however, overstated the matter by seeing both prodosis and apodosis as *vaticinia ex eventu*: "Die Jünger werden einst schweigen, weil der Widerstand der Judenshaft jedes Bekenntnis zu Jesus unmöglich macht, und dann werden an ihr nächste Wort redet: dann werden die Steine des zerstörten Jerusalem verkünden das der Christu zu ihn kam and von ihm verworfen wurde."

22. See Isa. 29:3; 37:33; Ezek. 4:1–3; 21:22; Jer. 52:4–5; Ps. 137: 7–9; 2 Sam. 17:13; 2 Kings 8:11.

23. So Gaston, pp. 359–60.

24. Septuagint, Jer. 5:14,19; 7:13; 16:11; 19:4; 22:9; 23:38; 27:7; and 38:20.

25. Hans Conzelmann, *The Theology of St. Luke,* trans. Geoffrey Buswell (New York: Harper & Row, 1960), p. 78.

26. See Brevard S. Childs, *The Book of Exodus* (Philadelphia: Westminster Press, 1974), pp. 170–75.

27. Without belaboring the point of the use of the "divine passive," one must view this text as an excellent illustration of the case in which mere human agency ("your enemies," v. 42) does not account adequately for the predicted events. Particularly the concept of the things that make for peace having been "hidden from your eyes" (v. 42), which is also the precondition of all that follows, requires the appeal to God as the source of judgment. See Isa. 29:14, where the Masoretic Text has the hithpael, "the discernment of their discerning shall be hid," and the Septuagint has the simple future active, "I shall hide [*krupsō*] the understanding of the understanding."

28. On the debate see Lars Hartmann, *Prophecy Interpreted,* Coniectanea Biblica, New Testament Series 1 (Lund: Gleerup, 1966), pp. 226–35. I. H. Marshall, *Commentary on Luke* (Grand Rapids: Eerdmans, 1978), pp. 752–58. Conzelmann, *The Theology of St. Luke,* pp. 125–36.

29. Norman Petersen, *Literary Criticism for New Testament Critics,* Guides to Biblical Scholarship (Philadelphia: Fortress Press, 1978), p. 83.

30. On the literary function of the crowd as compared with the chorus in Greek tragedy, see J. de Zwaan, "Was the Book of Acts a Posthumous Edition?" *Harvard Theological Review* 17 (1924):102.

31. Georg Braumann, "Die Lukanische Interpretation der Zerstörung Jerusalems," *Novum Testamentum* 6 (1963):120–27.

32. The phrase might be more adequately described as a midrashic "enrichment" of Joel from Isa. 2:2. But contrary to Ernst Haenchen, (*The Acts of the Apostles* [Philadelphia: Westminster Press, 1971], p. 179), who on theological grounds follows the Vaticanus manuscript which harmonizes Acts 2:27 to Joel 3:1, this variation must be acknowledged as consistent with Luke's eschatology. See Dodd, *According to the Scriptures,* p. 61, "we have reason to believe that the unit of reference was sometimes wider than the usually brief form of words actually quoted," and pp. 62–63 on Joel in Acts 2.

33. See especially the connections between Amos 9:13–14 and Joel 3–4 on the subject of restoration, and see Acts 15:16–17 discussed below.

34. On the place of the healing in Acts 3 as an image of the restoration of Israel within Luke–Acts, see Dennis M. Hamm, "The Sign of Healing" (Ph.D. diss.: St. Louis University, 1975), pp. 220–22, and pp. 163–74, where Hamm makes a clear case that "Luke presents the end-time restoration as beginning to unfold in the times of Jesus and the church" (p. 173). See also Arthur W. Wainwright, "Luke and the Restoration of the Kingdom to Israel," *Expository Times* 89 (1977:76–79.

35. The translation of *kataloipoi* as "those who remain" is perhaps the closest that Luke can be shown to come to a "remnant" theology.

36. See E. Earle Ellis, *Eschatology in Luke,* Facet Books, Biblical Series 30 (Philadelphia: Fortress Press, 1972). Henry J. Cadbury, "Acts and Eschatology," *The Background of the New Testament and Its Eschatology,* Studies in Honor of C. H. Dodd, ed. W. D. Davies (Cambridge: Cambridge University Press, 1956), pp. 300–21.

37. See Dodd, "The Fall of Jerusalem," pp. 76–78.

38. See F. Flücklinger, "Luke 21:20–24 und die Zerstörung Jerusalem," *Theologische Zeitschrift* 28 (1972):385–90.

39. See Marshall, *Commentary on Luke,* p. 773.

40. On Acts 28 see chapter 4 below. See also Dodd, "The Fall of Jerusalem," p. 79: "To a Christian reader—at least one acquainted with Paul's theology—the 'fulfillment of the times of the Gentiles' might suggest the progress of Gentile Christianity (cf. Rom. 11:25–26). But no such idea has influenced Luke's text, where we have, without any modi-

fication, the prophetic conception of Gentile oppression of the Holy City in retribution for its sins." See Thomas M. Raitt, *A Theology of Exile: Judgment/Deliverance in Jeremiah and Ezekiel* (Philadelphia: Fortress Press, 1977).

41. Trans. R. H. Charles, *The Pseudepigrapha of the Old Testament* (Oxford: Clarendon Press, 1913), p. 517.

42. See chapter 2, note 66.

43. See Robinson, "Luke, Gospel of," p. 559, and F. O. Francis, "Eschatology and History in Luke–Acts," *Journal of the American Academy of Religion* 37 (1969):49–63.

44. See note 34 above.

45. See 2 Baruch 68, note 41 above, and Plutarch "On the Delays of Divine Vengeance," chapter 1, note 9 above.

46. Compare this stern view of divine vengeance with the more gentle image of Wisdom 11 where God does punish but also "dost overlook men's sins that they may repent" (v. 23; see Acts 17:30), but the logic is the same. Josephus, however, is unpersuaded that "God still remains with his household in their iniquity" (*War* 5.413).

47. See Luke 12:35–48; 13:6–8; 19:11–27, 20:9–18; 21:29–36.

Chapter 4—The Messiah Must Die

1. Shemaryahu Talmon, "The Old Testament Text," *Qumran and the History of the Biblical Text,* ed. Frank Moore Cross and Shemaryahu Talmon (Cambridge, Mass.: Harvard University Press, 1975), pp. 10–11.

2. See the literature cited in chapter 1, notes 28–31.

3. See Lloyd Gaston, as cited in chapter 3, note 6 above.

4. Walter E. Pilgrim, "The Death of Christ in Lukan Soteriology" (Ph.D. diss.: Princeton Theological Seminary, 1971), pp. 74, 369.

5. In a penetrating analysis of "Jesus' Death in Lucan Soteriology" by Richard Zehnle in *Theological Studies* 30 (1969):420–44, this lively sociopolitical view of salvation was spotted (see especially pp. 439, 443). But most of the article was still devoted to the contrast with Paul arising from a rather individualized question: "How according to Luke is man saved, and what relation does the death of Jesus have to this salvation?" (p. 420).

6. See Eric Franklin, *Christ the Lord* (Philadelphia: Westminster Press, 1975).

7. Schuyler Brown, *Apostasy and Perseverance in the Theology of Luke,* Analecta Biblica 36 (Rome: Pontifical Biblical Institute, 1969), p. 123.

8. b. Baba Mezia 59b, trans. David L. Dungan, *Sourcebook of Texts for the Comparative Study of the Gospels,* 3d ed., ed. David L. Dungan

and David R. Cartlidge, SBL Sources for Biblical Study 1 (Missoula: Scholars Press, 1973), pp. 67–68.

9. Paul Schubert, "The Structure and Significance of Luke 24," *Neutestamentliche Studien für Rudolf Bultmann*, ZNW Beiheft 21 (Berlin: Töpelmann, 1954), p. 176.

10. Lloyd Gaston, *No Stone on Another: Studies in the Significance of the Fall of Jerusalem in the Synoptic Gospels*, Supplements to *Novum Testamentum* 23 (Leiden: E. J. Brill, 1970), p. 292.

11. See Henry J. Cadbury, "The Titles of Jesus in Acts," *The Beginings of Christianity*, ed. Kirsopp Lake and Henry J. Cadbury, vol. 5 (London: Macmillan, 1933), p. 366. Morna Hooker, *Jesus and the Servant* (Cambridge: Cambridge University Press, 1959), p. 110.

12. See Cadbury, "The Titles of Jesus in Acts," pp. 369–70, and Schubert, "The Structure and Significance of Luke 24."

13. William Stephen Kurz, *"The Function of Christological Proof from Prophecy for Luke and Justin"* (Ph.D. diss.: Yale University 1976), p. 77: "So in Luke–Acts, Jesus is anointed Christ, Lord and son of God by the Spirit but is not enthroned as such until his resurrection." Kurz's study is an excellent contribution to the interpretation of Luke–Acts, particularly as it grapples with the observation that "proof from prophecy arises out of a religious situation in which there are rival claims to the prophecies in a prophetic religion" (p. 148) and demonstrates Luke's acquaintance with and use of conventional rhetorical arguments. But the hypothesis that Luke's narrative intends to legitimate gentile Christianity as the heir of the prophecies and justify the turn of the Christian mission from Jews to Gentiles (see pp. 14, 91) is disputed in this volume.

14. See ibid., p. 117.

15. See ibid., pp. 129–30, J. de Zwaan, "Was the Book of Acts a Posthumous Edition?" *Harvard Theological Review* 17 (1924):102.

16. See Arthur Wallace Pickard-Cambridge, "Tragedy, Greek," *The Oxford Classical Dictionary* (Oxford: Clarendon Press, 1949), p. 918: "The play concluded with a final scene (*exodus*) very variable in structure; but there was never a great choral finale, like that of a modern oratorio; the chorus at most speak a few quiet words."

17. Reinhold Niebuhr, *Beyond Tragedy* (New York: Scribner's, 1937), pp. 160, 167.

18. Note, for example, the famous comparison between Psalm 8 and Sophocles' *Antigone* 332–75. See also Richmond Y. Hathorn, *Tragedy, Myth and Mystery* (Bloomington: Indiana University Press, 1962: Midland ed., 1966), p. 30: "In what ways are human beings implicated in the mystery of justice, and in what ways are they, bound as they are, blind to its workings?" See the objection of William C. Greene against the caricature that all Greek tragedy is fatalistic: "What is true is that a part, great or small, of the action in most of the plays is considered

to proceed from causes beyond the control of the characters." W. C. Greene, *Moira* (Cambridge, Mass.: Harvard University Press, 1944), p. 91.

19. Brown, *Apostasy and Perseverance,* pp. 81–92. Note Brown's persuasive argument that Peter's denial does not rupture the continuity of the faith or testimony of the disciples. It can be distinguished from the apostasy of Judas.

20. Paul W. Walaskay, "The Trial and Death of Jesus in the Gospel of Luke." *Journal of Biblical Literature* 94 (1975):81–93.

21. See 2 *Macc.* 9:5–29 on Antiochus and Josephus's *Antiquities* 19.343–53 on Herod Agrippa.

22. So also Martin Dibelius, *From Tradition to Gospel* (London: Scribner, 1935), p. 199: "the scene before Herod, quite unessential to the process of the trial, is interpolated because the friendship between Pilate and Herod (Luke 22:12) was read into Psalm 2:1–2."

23. See Jerome Kodell, "Luke's Use of *laos,* 'People,' Especially in the Jerusalem Narrative (Lk. 19, 28–24, 53)," *Catholic Biblical Quarterly* 31 (1969):327–43. The effort to distinguish too sharply between the *laos* and the *ochlos* may, however, be counterproductive to Kodell's insight. It is more important to observe Luke's careful identification of the composition of the *ochlos.*

24. On the other hand, it is worth noting that Luke has nothing of Matthew's phrase, "His blood be on us and on our children" (Matt. 27:25).

25. Greene, *Moira,* p. 102.

26. Mark's more cumbersome transition (15:37–39) with the intervening rending of the temple veil at least serves as a literary contrast since Mark must explain that the centurion had seen 'that thus he had expired."

27. See the oracle of Caiaphas in John 11:49–52.

28. So Walter Grundmann, *Das Evangelium nach Lukas,* Theologischer Handkommentar zum NT (Berlin: Evangelische Verlagsanstalt, 1966³), pp. 435–36.

29. See Josephus *War* 6.300–9 as discussed in chapter 3, note 3 above.

30. Lines 1169–70, 1182–85 translated by David Grene, *Sophocles I: The Complete Greek Tragedies,* ed. David Grene and Richard Lattimore (Chicago: University of Chicago Press, 1954), pp. 62–63.

31. See Edwyn Hoskyns and Noel Davey, *The Riddle of the New Testament* (London: Faber and Faber, 1958, 1931¹).

32. Of course, the hermeneutics of Qumran are still very much alive and well in certain circles generally regarded as sectarian by people who write and read books such as this one, especially if they read footnotes.

33. Not that all collections or cycles of Jesus' traditions reflect the

same coherence. Even the types and forms of the presynoptic collections (miracle stories, revelation discourses, logia, etc.) may display discrete Christological and hermeneutical options that develop into full-blown denominational positions in the second century. See Helmut Koester, "One Jesus and Four Primitive Gospels," *Trajectories through Early Christianity*, James M. Robinson and Helmut Koester (Philadelphia: Fortress Press, 1971), pp. 158–204. David L. Tiede, "Religious Propaganda and the Gospel Literature of the Early Christian Mission," due to appear in *Aufstieg und Niedergang der römischen Welt*, vol. 16 (Berlin: de Gruyter, –).

34. See James A. Sanders, *God Has a Story Too* (Philadelphia: Fortress Press, 1979), pp. 1–27.

35. See the critique of Jervell in Stephen G. Wilson, *The Gentiles and the Gentile Mission*, SNTSMS 23 (Cambridge: Cambridge University Press, 1973), pp. 226–33.

36. Ernst Haenchen, "The Book of Acts as Source Material for the History of Early Christianity," *Studies in Luke–Acts*, ed. Leander E. Keck and J. Louis Martyn (Philadelphia: Fortress Press, 1980), p. 278.

37. See Joachim Gnilka, *Die Verstockung Israels: Isaias 6:9–10 in der Theologie der Synoptiker*, Studien zum Alten und Neuen Testaments 3 (Munich: Kösel Verlag, 1961), pp. 13–18. See also Mark 4:12//Luke 8:10.

38. See also William J. Larkin, "The Old Testament Background of Luke xxii 43–44," *New Testament Studies* 25 (1979):250–54. J. Duncan M. Derrett, "Midrash in the New Testament: The Origin of Luke XXII 67–68," *Studia Theologica* 29 (1975):147–56. Donald Juel, "The Image of the Servant-Christ in the New Testament," *Southwestern Journal of Theology* 21 (1979):7–22: "The striking differences between the New Testament and the targumic interpretations of Isaiah 53 derive from prior conceptions. The targumist reads the Isaiah passage in the light of a traditional Jewish picture of the Messiah; Christians come to the text with a very different messianic conception modeled after Jesus the Messiah. Christians were no less careful in their exegesis, no less concerned about words and verbal associations than their contemporaries. What permitted them to find in the servant poems potentially useful christological material was the verbal link between 'servant' and 'Messiah.' "

Chapter 5—Fear Not, Little Flock

1. See Martin Braun, *History and Romance in Graeco-Oriental Literature* (Oxford: Blackwell, 1938), p. 3: "This popular narrative literature is the spiritual bread without which no proud people can stand the pres-

sure of alien domination, and it is individual heroic figures in whom the feeling and longing of the masses come to a concentrated expression."

2. On the terms *"asphalia"* and *"parrēsia,"* as thematic to Luke–Acts, see Paul S. Minear, "Dear Theo: The Kerygmatic Intention and Claim of the Book of Acts," *Interpretation* 27 (1973):131–50.

3. Trans. R. H. Charles, *The Pseudepigrapha of the Old Testament,* pp. 523, 579.

4. See George W. MacRae, "Whom Heaven Must Receive Until the Time: Reflections on the Christology of Acts," *Interpretation* 27 (1973): 151–65.

5. Points of comparison and contrast with other early Christian efforts to define Christian identity and faith from within as well as over against other Jewish views and practices have been identified in several recent studies and invite further research. See specially: Krister Stendahl, *Paul among Jews and Gentiles* (Philadelphia: Fortress Press, 1976); O. Lamar Cope, *Matthew: A Scribe Trained for the Kingdom of Heaven,* CBQMS 5 (Washington, D.C.: Catholic Biblical Association, 1976); and Raymond E. Brown, " 'Other Sheep Not of This Fold'; The Johannine Perspective on Christian Diversity in the Late First Century," *Journal of Biblical Literature* 97 (1978):5–22.

6. See Frederick W. Danker, *Luke,* Proclamation Commentaries, ed. Gerhard Krodel (Philadelphia: Fortress Press, 1976), especially pp. 6–8.

Selected Bibliography

Anderson, Hugh. "Broadening Horizons: The Rejection at Nazareth Pericope of Luke 4:16–30 in Light of Recent Critical Trends." *Interpretation* 18 (1964):259–75.

Baltzer, Klaus. "The Meaning of the Temple in the Lukan Writings." *Harvard Theological Review* 58 (1965):263–77.

Barrett, C. K. *Luke the Historian in Recent Study.* Facet Books, Biblical Series, 24. Philadelphia: Fortress Press, 1970.

Braumann, G. "Die lukanische Interpretation der Zerstörung Jerusalems." *Novum Testamentum* 6 (1963):120–27.

Brown, Raymond E. *The Birth of the Messiah.* Garden City, N.Y.: Doubleday, 1977.

Cadbury, Henry J. *The Making of Luke–Acts.* London: SPCK, 1961 (first published 1927).

Cadbury, Henry J. *The Style and Literary Method of Luke.* Harvard Theological Studies, 6. Cambridge, Mass.: Harvard University Press, 1920.

Conzelmann, Hans. *The Theology of St. Luke.* Translated by Geoffrey Buswell. London: Farber and Farber, 1960.

Crockett, Larrimore C. "Luke 4:25–27 and Jewish-Gentile Relations in Luke–Acts." *Journal of Biblical Literature* 88 (1969):177–83.

Crockett, Larrimore C. "The Old Testament in the Gospel of Luke." Doctoral dissertation, Brown University, 1961.

Dahl, Nils A. "A People for His Name (Acts 15:4)." *New Testament Studies* 4 (1957):319–27.

Dahl, Nils A. "The Purpose of Luke–Acts." *Jesus in the Memory of the Early Church,* pp. 87–98. Minneapolis: Augsburg Publishing House, 1976.

Danker, Frederick W. *Jesus and the New Age.* St. Louis: Clayton Publishing House, 1972.

153

Danker, Frederick W. *Luke.* Proclamation Commentaries, edited by Gerhard Krodel. Philadelphia: Fortress Press, 1976.

Dodd, C. H. *According to the Scriptures: The Sub-Structure of New Testament Theology.* Digswell Place: James Nisbet, 1952.

Dodd, C. H. "The Fall of Jerusalem and the 'Abomination of Desolation.'" *Journal of Roman Studies* 37 (1947):47–54. Reprinted in *More New Testament Studies,* pp. 69–83. Manchester: Manchester University Press, 1968.

Evans, C. F. "The Central Section of St. Luke's Gospel." *Studies in the Gospels.* Essays in Memory of R. H. Lightfoot, edited by D. E. Nineham, pp. 37–53. Oxford: Blackwell, 1955.

Foakes Jackson, F. J., and Lake, Kirsopp. *The Beginnings of Christianity.* 5 vols. London: Macmillan, 1920–1933.

Franklin, Eric. *Christ the Lord.* Philadelphia: Westminster Press, 1975.

Gaston, Lloyd. *No Stone on Another: Studies in the Significance of the Fall of Jerusalem in the Synoptic Gospels.* Supplements to *Novum Testamentum,* 23. Leiden: E. J. Brill, 1970.

Gill, David. "Observations on the Lukan Travel Narrative and Some Related Passages." *Harvard Theological Review* 63 (1970):199–221.

Hamm, M. Dennis. "The Sign of Healing: Acts 3:1–10, a Study in Lucan Theology." Ph.D. dissertation, St. Louis University, 1975.

Heschel, Abraham J. *The Prophets.* New York: Harper & Row, 1962.

Hooker, Morna D. *Jesus and the Servant.* Cambridge: Cambridge University Press, 1959.

Hultgren, Arland J. "Interpreting the Gospel of Luke." *Interpretation* 30 (1976):353–65.

Jervell, Jacob. *Luke and the People of God.* Minneapolis: Augsburg Publishing House, 1972.

Johnson, Luke T. *The Literary Function of Possessions in Luke–Acts.* SBLDS, 39. Missoula: Scholars Press, 1977.

Karris, Robert J. "Missionary Communities: A New Paradigm for the Study of Luke–Acts." *Catholic Biblical Quarterly* 41 (1979):80–97.

Karris, Robert J. *What Are They Saying about Luke and Acts?: A Theology of the Faithful God.* New York: Paulist Press, 1979.

Keck, Leander E., and Martyn, J. Louis, eds. *Studies in Luke–Acts.* Essays presented in honor of Paul Schubert. Philadelphia: Fortress Press, 1980.

Klein, Charlotte. *Anti-Judaism in Christian Theology.* Translated by Edward Quinn. Philadelphia: Fortress Press, 1978.

Kodell, Jerome. "Luke's Use of *laos,* 'People,' especially in the Jerusalem Narrative (Lk 19,28–24,53)." *Catholic Biblical Quarterly* 31 (1969):327–43.

Kurz, William Stephen "The Function of Christological Proof from

Prophecy for Luke and Justin." Ph.D. dissertation, Yale University, 1976.

Lohse, Eduard. "Lukas als Theologe der Heilsgeschichte." *Evangelische Theologie* 14 (1954):256–76.

Mack, Burton. "Imitatio Mosis: Patterns of Cosmology and Soteriology in the Hellenistic Synagogue." *Studia Philonica* 1 (1972):27–55.

Mack, Burton. "Wisdom Myth and Mythology." *Interpretation* 24 (1970):46–60.

MacRae, George W. "Whom Heaven Must Receive until the Time." *Interpretation* 27 (1973):151–65.

Minear, Paul S. "Dear Theo: The Kerygmatic Intention and Claim of the Book of Acts." *Interpretation* 27 (1973):131–50.

Minear, Paul S. "Luke's Use of the Birth Stories." *Studies in Luke–Acts,* edited by Leander E. Keck and J. Louis Martyn, pp. 111–30. Philadelphia: Fortress Press, 1980.

Neusner, Jacob. *A Life of Yohanan ben Zakkai.* 2d ed. Leiden: E. J. Brill, 1970.

Pervo, Richard. "The Literary Genre of the Acts of the Apostles." Ph.D. dissertation, Harvard University, 1979.

Pohlenz, M. *Freedom in Greek Life and Thought.* Dordrecht: D. Reidel, 1966.

Robinson, W. C., Jr. "Luke, Gospel of." *The Interpreter's Dictionary of the Bible.* Supplementary Vol., pp. 558–60. Nashville: Abingdon Press, 1976.

Sanders, James A. "The Ethic of Election in Luke's Great Banquet Parable." *Essays in Old Testament Ethics.* J. Philip Hyatt, In Memoriam, edited by James L. Crenshaw and John T. Willis, pp. 245–71. New York: KTAV, 1974.

Sanders, James A. "From Isaiah 61 to Luke 4." *Christianity, Judaism, and Other Greco-Roman Cults.* Studies for Morton Smith at Sixty. Part One: New Testament, edited by Jacob Neusner, pp. 75–106. Leiden: E. J. Brill, 1975.

Schubert, Paul. "The Structure and Significance of Luke 24." *Neutestamentliche Studien für Rudolf Bultmann,* ZNW Beiheft 21, pp. 165–86. Berlin: Töpelmann, 1954.

Schürmann, Heinz. *Das Lukasevangelium,* I. Herder's Theologischer Kommentar, III. Freiburg: Herder, 1969.

Schütz, Frieder. *Der leidende Christus: Die angefochtene Gemeinde und das Christuskerygma der lukanischen Schriften.* Beiträge zur Wissenschaft vom Alten und Neuen Testament, 9. Stuttgart: Kohlhammer, 1968.

Steck, O. H. *Israel und das gewaltsame Geschick der Propheten.* WMANT, 23. Neukirchen: Neukirchener Verlag, 1967.

Talbert, Charles H. *Literary Patterns, Theological Themes and the Genre of Luke–Acts.* SBLMS, 20. Missoula: Scholars Press, 1975.

Talbert, Charles H. "Shifting Sands: The Recent Study of the Gospel of Luke." *Interpretation* 30 (1976):381–95.

Thompson, Alden Lloyd. *Responsibility for Evil in the Theodicy of IV Ezra.* SBLDS, 29. Missoula: Scholars Press, 1977.

Vermes, Geza. "Bible and Midrash: Early Old Testament Exegesis." *The Cambridge History of the Bible,* I, pp. 199–231. Cambridge: Cambridge University Press, 1970.

Wainwright, Arthur W. "Luke and the Restoration of the Kingdom of Israel." *Expository Times* 89 (1977):76–79.

Wilckens, Ulrich. *Die Missionsreden der Apostelgeschichte.* WMAN1, 5. Neukirchen-Vluyn: Neukirchener Verlag, 1963.

Wilson, S. G. *The Gentiles and the Gentile Mission in Luke–Acts.* SNTS Monographs, 23. New York: Cambridge University Press, 1973.

Winston, David S. "Freedom and Determinism in Greek Philosophy and Jewish Hellenistic Wisdom." *Studia Philonica* 2 (1973):40–50.

Zehnle, Richard. "The Salvific Character of Jesus' Death in Lucan Soteriology." *Theological Studies* 30 (1969):420–44.

Ziesler, J. A. "Luke and the Pharisees." *New Testament Studies* 25 (1978–1979):146–57.

Index of Names

157

Index of References to Primary Texts

I. OLD TESTAMENT AND APOCRYPHA

159

II. INTERTESTAMENTAL JEWISH SOURCES

III. NEW TESTAMENT AND EARLY CHURCH

IV. GREEK AND LATIN AUTHORS